"Dear Mom,
Send More Money!"

"Dear Mom, Send More Money!"

A Collection of Columns

by

Skippy Lawson

Edited by *Barbara Stinson*
and *Dahlia Wren*

With a Foreword by *Bill Boyd*

Seawinds Press

Published by Seawinds Press
P. O. Box 5469
Macon, Georgia 31208-5469
Copyright © 1986 by Skippy Lawson

Portions of this book are also under copyright
by the *Macon Telegraph and News*

Columns in this book were first printed by the *Macon Telegraph and News* or the
Hawkinsville Dispatch and News and are reprinted here with permission.

Jacket design by Lanny Webb.

Manufactured in the United States of America.

First Edition.

Library of Congress Catalog Card No.: 86-91103.
ISBN 0-9616375-1-X

For my Father and Mother,

LLOYD AND SYDNEY DAVIS,

Who have always encouraged me in my writing,

and for my children,

SABRA, NANCY AND HARLEY,

Who have given me so many things to write about.

Contents

*Reprinted from the *Hawkinsville Dispatch and News.*

Foreword

Let's start this book with an exposé. The author of this book isn't really named Skippy Lawson. Skippy is a nickname, and Lawson is the name she took when she was married.

This book actually was written by Sydney Shipley Davis. I know that doesn't sound like a woman's name. And it must come as a shocking revelation to those who don't know her real name. But it's true.

Both Sydney and Shipley are fourth generation family names, and Davis, of course, was her maiden name.

The nickname she chose has not spared her a masculine name-image, even though her femininity should be obvious to the most casual observer. She often gets mail addressed to Mr. Skippy Lawson, and just recently, a clerk at the tag office watched her sign her real given name and then informed Skippy that, "Your husband will have to sign his own name."

Well, so much for the exposé. Now let me tell you a little about this talented journalist whose wit and words often remind me of the great Erma Bombeck.

Sydney Shipley Davis grew up in Atlanta. Without knowledge of the peace and tranquility of life in the countryside, she remained there to go to college, earning a degree in history from Emory University.

She left Atlanta at the age of 23, married and headed for life in the slow lane in Hawkinsville—which has only two lanes, both of them very slow.

For about eight years she was a homemaker, raising three children: daughters Sabra and Nancy and son Harley. Her life changed when she gained financial interest in the *Hawkinsville Dispatch and News* in 1974. Until that time, she'd never considered a newspaper writing career.

I met Skippy that year. She was the editor of the paper, and I was traveling around Middle Georgia for the *Macon Telegraph and News*. It didn't take long for me to learn that, in spite of majoring in history in college, newspapering was her strong suit. It seemed that every time I went to the Georgia Press Convention, here came Skippy down the aisle gathering up awards by the armload. In three years at the weekly paper, she won three first-place awards for column writing, a job we both love and hate.

Even those who are used to reading Skippy's weekly column in the *Telegraph and News* are going to find a lot of new reading in this book because her early columns appeared only in the Hawkinsville newspaper.

After she came to work for the *Telegraph and News* in 1977, Skippy established a bureau in Dublin, reporting everything from courts to club news. Her fairness in reporting and gentle touch with features about everyday folks built a Skippy Lawson fan club that's still going strong.

In Macon, she ran the state news service for a year and then switched to the feature department. And she soon returned to writing a weekly column.

She started making those trips to pick up awards again. She won two national awards—a second-place award from the National Society of Newspaper Columnists and a first-place award from the National League of American Pen Women. Her column also placed in the top three in both serious and humorous categories of Georgia Press Association competition in 1982 and again in 1985.

I guarantee that you'll like Skippy's return to the fast lane of rearing three teen-age children, single parenting and holding down a full-time writing job. She'll make you laugh, but there are a few lumps for the throat in this book, too.

A few of these columns are about her childhood. But mostly, they're about rearing three children and coping with life—and cats—at home.

One of my favorites—a priceless melodrama that only a young mother can know—tells about bringing home her first child and worrying about everything from hiccups to falling-out hair. And with her rare touch of humor, she takes you right on through the kids' recent years when they keep writing from college, "Dear Mom, send more money!"

I haven't reached the send-more-money stage with my son Joe, so I'm keeping a copy of this book close at hand to help guide me—with a smile on my face, like hers.

Happy reading!

Bill Boyd
Columnist
Macon Telegraph and News

Acknowledgements

To my editors Barbara Stinson and DahliaWren, jacket designer Lanny Webb and photographer Danny Gilleland for their time and creativity; to *Macon Telegraph and News* Publisher Ed Olson, General Manager Billy Watson and Editor Rick Thomas and to *Hawkinsville Dispatch and News* Publisher Charlie Southerland; to Carr Dodson, Buddy Haggard and Bo Whaley for invaluable advice; and to Bill Boyd, who said to me one day, "Why don't you publish a book?" —

Thank you

Out of the Cradle
and into Absolutely Everything

*This nation has millions of people who are both clever
and fearless. Most of them are 4.*

—anon.

Having three babies under 3 years old gave a whole new meaning to the phrase "rock around the clock." People stopped me everywhere—on the street corner, in the grocery store and at the doctor's office—and I found my eyes glazing over as I answered two questions again and again, "Yes, they're all mine," and, "No, they're not triplets."

Some of these columns were written at the time; others were written in retrospect. In all of them, you'll probably notice that, for Mom, the patter of little feet provided quite an education.

Sleep, Baby, Sleep— Please!

How well I recall the first afternoon at home with my first baby.

The baby's doctor probably recalls it, too.

I grew up in a family of few babies. For that reason, I regarded my new little person with a good bit of anxiety, afraid I might break her.

My initial fear was that she would quit breathing. I shouldn't have worried. She had healthy lungs, which she proceeded to exercise whenever I tried to put her down.

As long as I held her, she was content. I began to envision carrying this demanding little bundle constantly in my arms day and night until she learned to walk. The prospect made me very nervous.

I called the doctor.

"You didn't tell me she would cry every time I put her down," I told him.

He was patient. Babies cry, he reminded me. He suggested I let her cry for a few minutes and see whether she would then drop off to sleep. Or, he said, try rocking her.

We rocked. For miles. Finally, reluctantly, the little lids closed, fluttered open again and then shut tight.

For a few minutes I sat there, admiring the round head, the silky black hair, the tiny fingers. Then I tiptoed to the baby bed and softly put her down. She stretched a little and then settled down to sleep, her diapered bottom poked up in the air.

This wasn't so bad, I decided as I tiptoed away. I put on the coffeepot, thinking a cup would fortify me before I tackled the job of mixing formula—a scientific first. What if I poisoned her?

Just as I got the coffee ready, I heard her tuning up again. She had been asleep all of 10 minutes. Leaving the coffee to turn stone cold, I rushed to her room.

It was when I picked her up that I saw the horrifying calamity. Her hair was falling out! There was a big smudge of hair on the sheet where her head had been. Home only an hour, and already my baby was coming apart!

I rushed to the phone. "Her hair is falling out," I shrieked. "It's all over the sheet."

The doctor was patient. Newborns lose their first hair and soon grow a new batch, he told me. There was nothing to worry about. He suggested I calm down and give her a bottle.

After half an hour of testing the baby bottle, splashing most of the formula on my wrist to make sure it was not too hot or cold, I ventured to feed her.

Holding the baby carefully so that her head wouldn't fall off, I tilted the bottle and poked the nipple into her mouth. Nothing. She wouldn't suck. I twisted it around and shook it a little. She yawned and turned her head away.

My baby wouldn't eat! I ran to the phone and dialed the doctor's number.

"Maybe she's not hungry," he suggested, something I hadn't thought of. His measured tone suggested deliberate patience. "Why don't you wait and try again in about an hour?"

Sure enough, an hour later she showed great interest in the bottle, draining it in just a few minutes. I put her on my shoulder and patted her on the back, "bringing up the bubble" as my grandmother used to say.

Dutifully, she bubbled. Then she began to hiccup. She looked startled as one hiccup after another racked her tiny frame. She was going to hiccup to death! Frantically, I jiggled her. More hiccups.

I ran to the telephone and called the doctor . . .

It was a very long afternoon.

First Day of School

When school opened this fall, a big change took place at our house. The baby entered first grade and seemed to grow up overnight.

He faced the first day of school with glee. Me, too. As do most parents, I had by the end of the summer developed a longing for the orderly, scheduled routine that school days bring. And with all the children in school, I looked forward to the 8:30 to 3:30 peace and quiet.

On the first school morning, he got dressed in his new clothes. (Why do we buy them new clothes for the first days of school? They always wear them once and go back to their faded summertime cut-offs and T-shirts.)

He arrived in the kitchen for breakfast looking very shiny and more presentable than I had seen him in three months.

He had brushed his hair and his teeth without being told and had even washed his face. His shirt was right-side-out instead of the usual. His shoes were tied. Both of them. Even through my early morning stupor—I am never completely awake before noon—I was amazed.

"Now that I'm in first grade, I'm not going to call you mama anymore, Mother," he informed me through a mouthful of toast. That was two weeks ago. He hasn't called me mama since.

Armed with his new pencil case and first grader's writing pad—the kind with alternating dotted and solid lines—he waited impatiently by the door. He was so anxious to go that if he had had his way, we would have arrived at the school about 7:30.

Since it was his very first day, I let the little girls go ahead on the school bus while I drove him in the car.

On the way, he became very silent. His eyes were enormous.

"Why are you sitting on your hands?" I asked him.

"So I won't suck my thumb," he replied with candor.

Realizing that I had an acute case of stage fright on my hands, I began an enthusiastic commentary on school—how nice the teachers would be, what good food in the lunchroom, how much fun to make so many new friends and the interesting new games he would learn at recess.

He absorbed this in total silence.

Once in the school room, he replied to all his teacher's pleasant over-tures in reluctant, whispered monosyllables, clinging to my hand and showing great interest in his shoes. As the teacher turned to greet some other children, I began to question him in what I realized was a phony, enthusiastic-mother voice.

No, he didn't like the cute little desks.

No, he didn't see anybody he knew.

No, he didn't think it was going to be any fun at all.

No, he didn't want to learn any new things.

All this was conveyed by emphatic, negative shakes of his head.

But then he spotted a little boy he remembered from kindergarten last year. After a few false starts, he summoned all his courage and crossed the room to talk with his friend. In just a few minutes, he was back, tugging on my hand. I leaned down, thinking he was going to ask where the bath-room was.

"Mother," he whispered, "when you leave, don't kiss me goodbye, OK?"

The Pilgrims:
A Progressive People

A young child labored long and thoughtfully over a Thanksgiving composition one November school day many years ago.

An amused teacher sent it to me, and the much erased and penciled-over paper is among the things I cherish.

I present it here so that we all may remember that the freedom we enjoy so blithely is rooted in the courage and faith of a hardy band who suffered much and were thankful anyway.

The First Thanksgiving

The first Thanksgiving was held somewhere up north by a group of famous people known as The Pilgrims. They wore black suits with square white collars and silver buckles that made them look different from the Catholics who dressed normal.

The Pilgrims were some of the first people to ever come to the United States, and that was the beginning.

They floated over here on a big ship called the *Mayflower* because they were tired of the king of England chopping off their heads. A lot of them died on the way because of storms. The *Mayflower* sank several times a day, and they called it a hardship.

But they made it, and the voyage became known as the Pilgrim's Progress.

When they saw land they were happy because they knew they didn't have to be seasick anymore. Besides, some of their bread had gotten worms in it. Yuck.

When they came to a big rock, they stopped and got off the boat and named the rock Plymouth Rock. It is still there today, and you can see it if you go there. Plymouth Rock was named for a car, and my granddaddy has one.

At that time, the United States was mostly woods, and Indians lived there with turkeys and maize, which was really corn but they called it maize because maize is Indian for corn.

The Pilgrims cut down trees and built houses on Plymouth Rock and that was the first town. It was called Plymouth Colony.

Some of the Indians were friendly and shared their corn with the Pilgrims. They also showed the Pilgrims how to shoot turkeys with bows and arrows.

To be friendly, too, the Pilgrims showed the Indians how to hunt with guns, which was very fascinating to the Indians because they had never shot a gun before. Or ever even seen one.

The Pilgrims called their guns muskets, and instead of bullets they shot them with powder. The Pilgrim ladies did not believe in wearing powder on their faces, so they shot guns with it instead. No lipstick either.

The Pilgrims were very happy because they were out from under persecution. And except for dying in the wintertime because of freezes and getting smallpox, which was a terrible disease you caught from mosquito bites that itched, they were glad to be in the United States. They called it the land of plenty because everywhere you looked there was plenty of everything.

And one day after they raised some crops, they decided there was too much for just them to eat by theirselves.

So, they decided to have a party and invite the Indians and thank God for it all. They called it the fruits of their labor even though it was really vegetables.

The Indians could come, and they got there early in the morning and brought presents like blankets and deer, and the Pilgrims thanked them even if they didn't think blankets were a very good present. Everyone had to be polite to each other because they didn't know each other very well, and they prayed a lot.

But they had fun, too, and played games and sang Thanksgiving songs like the national anthem.

Then the Pilgrims sat down at a table and the Indians sat on the ground because of no extra chairs, and they all had a square meal together.

It lasted a couple of days, and that was the first Thanksgiving. We have a picture of it in our history book. It looks pretty good, but our Thanksgivings are better now because we have learned how to cook more things, like sweet potatoes and cranberry sauce and pies. That's because our mothers have stoves, and the Pilgrim ladies had to cook in the fireplace or outside in a hole because they didn't know about kitchens in those days.

I think Thanksgiving is a very nice holiday because it gives you something to do before Christmas.

Off to Camp!

My firstborn child has just left for a week of 4-H camp. There is already an eerie sort of quiet around the house, even though the two younger children are noisily watching television.

Do parents always feel a wrench when a child leaves for several days, or is it just me?

There was such a bustle of getting ready yesterday.

"Where's my trunk key?"

"I want to pack everything myself so I won't forget anything."

"Don't let Nancy and Harley come in my room and mess with my things while I'm gone."

"I need more postage stamps." (They always take tons of stationery to camp and then usually write no letters.)

Hovering between childhood and adolescence, she had lined up her dolls and stuffed animals to watch as she packed her clothes, hair curlers and the only makeup she's allowed to use—lip gloss.

By 11 p.m. everything had been done, and she had gone off, unwillingly, to bed. The open trunk on the floor was jam-packed with clothes, sheets, her favorite books and numerous other items that "I might need at camp." These included a flashlight, extra blanket, a baseball cap and glove, snapshots of her horse (lest she forget what he looks like in a week's time) and several games "in case it rains."

I marveled at the pre-adolescent mind and made a mental note to ask her tomorrow morning whether she had remembered to pack her toothbrush.

This morning when I got up, she was already dressed and fidgeting.

"When are we leaving?"

"How much longer?"

"Isn't it time to go yet?"

Departure from the Extension Service office was a noisy one as friends called to each other and chose places on the buses. When the two buses filled with luggage and campers finally pulled out, all the mothers standing bravely on the sidewalk waved goodbye. Most of the campers were having such a fine time, they rode away without a backward glance or wave.

Returning home, I went to her room to survey the devastation. There were open drawers with clothes hanging out, the unmade bed, magazines strewn across the floor—and several surprises.

On the windowsill, alongside several glasses of cuttings was a note: "Please water my houseplants everyday."

On a shelf, she had lined up her collection of stuffed animals, and propped against the tiger was the order: "Do not move these animals."

On the door was tacked this grim warning: "Nancy and Harley stay out or else."

And hanging in the bathroom was her toothbrush.

17 Candles

Seventeen years ago this week, a nurse brought a baby into my hospital room and placed her next to me on the bed, wrapped like a papoose in a pink blanket.

She was 21 inches long and weighed 7½ pounds. She wouldn't want me to tell you what she weighs now, but at 17, she's considerably taller than 21 inches, taller even than her mother.

She was about one hour old when I got my first good look at her. Her eyes were new-baby blue, and what little hair she had was carefully combed into a single finger curl on the very top of her head.

Now that hair falls below her shoulders. She tells me that soon she will be taking Geritol now that she's 17, and she reminds me, round-eyed, that next year she will be an adult.

"Awesome," she says. It is awesome, and it makes me feel old and bent and withered and gray.

They say a baby's vision is blurry in the early weeks, but on that night she seemed to have everything in clear focus, and she didn't seem at all pleased with the day's events. I resolved on the spot to be a perfect mother.

Later, it turned out that her vision really was blurry after all. She went off to second grade proudly sporting new glasses, calling everyone's attention to them—frequently.

Lately, stronger glasses have taken their place. She wears them when she drives and when she reads. But she doesn't talk about them much, and she takes them off when a good-looking guy appears. Years make a great difference in what pleases us.

As I watched her that first night, the new baby opened her mouth and yawned—a huge, long yawn that squeezed her eyes shut. No teeth, of course. The teeth come later.

We've been through the baby teeth and the cutting of permanent teeth and the wearing of braces. Now, all those teeth she didn't have 17 years ago are straight, pearly white and expensive.

The nurse smiled and left us together. A small panic gathered in my breast. I had never been alone with a baby before. What if she cried? How to make her stop? I had a lot to learn.

In 17 years of parenting, one learns what to do when the baby cries. It's easy enough early in the game when an ice cream cone can restore the sunshine. It's harder later on. A kitten was hit by a car, and she viewed the still body tearfully, wanting to know where was the kitten's "alive." When she was older, a beloved great-aunt succumbed to cancer. The questions she asked then began with "why." Questions that begin with "why" are the hardest ones to answer.

But on that first night, she looked calm and sort of sleepy and not at all inclined to cry. My panic eased, and curiosity took its place.

On first glance, I marveled that a baby could look just like Sir Winston Churchill and still be perfectly beautiful.

She met my gaze levelly, and then her first frown gathered on her brow—a dreadful scowl that brought a deep crease just above her nose. That frown was so incongruous on the tiny face that I laughed out loud.

That same frown reappears from time to time. Within the family, we refer to it as her "dark look," and we leave her alone when it is dominant. It can indicate a broken date and hurt feelings, or it can simply be a frown of concentration when the algebra gets tough. At any rate, the crease above her nose is deepening annually. It will cause her some consternation when she is older.

On that first night, she would have fit comfortably in the crook of one arm, but it had been a long and arduous day for both of us. Instead of picking her up, I lay there at a small distance and gazed at the new little person.

She moved her arm beneath the blanket, so I loosened it for her, releasing a tiny fist. She waved it about and stuffed it into her mouth but not before I had time to wonder at the minute fingers and smooth nails the size of match heads.

Those nails, now shaped into long ovals, frequently painted, have become the objects of some vanity on her part. Vanity is not too large a sin for a young lady, I think, provided there is not too much of it. She willingly turns those well-tended hands to chauffeuring and errands for her working mother, so I am content that the vanity is balanced by a generosity of spirit.

I never did develop into the perfect parent. Sometimes I'll do or say something, and she'll say, "That's dumb, Mom," and it turns out usually that it is.

We've learned a lot, she and I, in the past 17 years.

Some Things Never Change

She was 5, and he was 3. She was bigger, and—till one long-ago afternoon—she was the boss. He was just a toddler who, on that day, happened onto a sure-fire way to get his big sister's goat. It has served him well ever since.

I heard her shriek with rage on that memorable afternoon and found her sitting on the floor, her mouth a big square, the tears dripping off her chin and soaking into the rug.

"He called me a dum-dum," she wailed. "Mommy, make him stop calling me a dum-dum."

"Dum-dum, dum-dum, dum-dum," chanted her baby brother, dancing around gleefully, pleased with his new-found power.

I grabbed him up just before she tried to club him with her toy telephone. And so, he survived a few more years.

She was 10, and he was 8. She was bigger and could run faster. He had become masterful in the role of pesky little brother.

I heard her shriek with rage one day and found her chasing him through the house, mad as a hornet, her pigtails flying.

"He called me a stupid, sissy girl," she screamed. "Mom, make him stop calling me a stupid, sissy girl, or I'm gonna pull out all his hair and bash his head in."

"Stu-pid, sis-sy gi-irl, stu-pid, sis-sy gi-irl," he chanted, hopping around gleefully.

I stepped between them just before she had a chance to club him with her catcher's mitt. And so, he survived a few more years.

She was 13, he was 11. She was heavier, taller and a tomboy who could climb trees faster than he and stole third base from him routinely. He was a ceaseless tease and by then proficient in the role of nuisance.

I heard her shriek with rage one day and found them in the living room, both screaming. He was screaming for help. She was so mad she was incoherent. She had wrestled him to the floor and was getting ready to punch him in the nose.

"He called me a little shrimpy twerp," she yelled by way of explanation, flailing her arms and kicking as I separated them. "Make him stop calling me a little shrimpy twerp."

"Lit-tle shrimp-y twer-rp, lit-tle shrimp-y twer-rp," he chanted, grinning and dancing just out of reach.

"I'll show him who's a little shrimpy twerp!" she raged. "I'm gonna beat him up and mash his nose in. I'm gonna smush him like a fly. I'm gonna break his arms and break his legs."

Once again I was able to save him—this time from being beaten up, mashed, smushed and broken. And so, he survived a few more years.

She's 18, and he's 16—almost. The tables have turned. She's petite, feminine and a college freshman. She's sweet as pie—usually. He's almost a foot taller, his voice is deep, and he walks around the house flexing his muscles. To her chagrin, he has assumed the role of big brother, telling her how to drive, criticizing her clothes and hair, passing judgment on her friends—all for her own good, of course.

One day recently, she flounced into my room, looking like a thundercloud, and flopped down on the foot of the bed. Tears of rage stood in her eyes, and a canary could have perched on her lower lip.

"He keeps calling me Babycakes, and he listens in when I'm on the telephone, and he tells all my friends to call me Babycakes, too. He even told me what time to come home from the party tonight," she wailed. "Mom, you've got to make him stop bossing me around and calling me Babycakes. Babycakes! What a stupid, idiotic name! I'm gonna beat him up, I'm gonna mash him, I'm gonna run over him, I'm gonna break his face—just as soon as I catch him."

He ambled into the room, grinning. "Who you gonna beat up, Babycakes?" he asked, patting her on the head indulgently and then dodging swiftly as she took a wild swing at him.

"Babycakes, Babycakes, Baa—by—cakes," he chanted as he ran for his life down the hall, his furious sister in pursuit.

Some things never change. When she's 70 and he's 68, he will probably still be baiting her with sassy names. But I'm not intervening anymore. They're both taller, younger and stronger than I am.

And I'd like to survive a few more years.

There is Hope—
Really!

All you mothers of diapered babies and toddling moppets out there, listen up.

Are your children messy eaters? Do you spend your life chanting a litany of "Quit mashing broccoli into the rug," "The TV screen is not for spreading butter" and "Don't blow bubbles in your milk"?

I have just discovered that there is hope. Read on and take heart.

Just in case you fear you are raising a tribe of permanently uncivilized savages who all their lives will pick their noses in public and eat off the bottoms of their shoes. . .

Just in case you're sure that at her college graduation your girl-child will still be carrying around that mouthful of oatmeal she's been holding all morning. . .

Just in case you suspect that at her bridesmaid's luncheon she will cry and pound her fork on the table, declaring that she hates yucky creamed chicken . . .

Just in case you know chimpanzees with better table manners . . .

There's hope.

Are your tabletops distressed with little peaks of congealed mashed potato?

Are your walls antiqued with streaks of splashed orange juice?

Is sandblasting the only method that appears likely to clean the dried squash and blueberries off your ceilings?

Do your children drink out of the dog's bowl? The toilet bowl?

There is hope.

I have stood where you are standing. I have anguished as little ones gleefully overturned plates and cups to watch the contents ooze and drip to the floor.

I have alternately raged and sobbed over tomato soup dumped into the toy chest and pancake syrup poured on the cat.

I have shrieked with crazed, hysterical laughter as I discovered petrified grits mashed into the little holes in the telephone receiver.

But there is hope.

A landmark event occurred last week, an event that lifted forever my 17-year suicidal depression.

My 17-year-old daughter sat at the kitchen table munching daintily on an ice cream cone, dabbing the corners of her mouth from time to time with a napkin.

She started to say something, then paused long enough to swallow first.

I was stunned. She used her napkin! She swallowed before speaking! For all those years, she had been listening after all.

Somewhere in a remote area of her brain all those desperate little phrases I had uttered—"Use your napkin," "Don't wipe your mouth on your sleeve," "Don't talk with your mouth full"—had been absorbed. Even though she had ignored them, at some level of her subconsciousness they had become imprinted.

Which means that the most hopeless case—a case that could have reduced Miss Manners to insane babbling—has turned out well.

Just consider: We're talking about the child who used to stash used lollipops in her socks for safekeeping. Sometimes her feet stuck together, and her lollipops were always coated with sock fuzz.

This is the child who wore her clothes wrong-side-out to nursery school to conceal indelible mustard and ketchup stains.

This is the child who once saved her hard-boiled Easter eggs by wedging them between the mattresses on her bed. The exterminator found them weeks later, flattened and totally disgusting, after I called him to come remove whatever had died in her room.

She got her jollies rubbing blobs of chocolate pudding in her hair.

I have seen her smiling happily in her high chair, her food bowl overturned on her head and rivers of strained beets dripping from her eyebrows and down her neck.

She entertained herself at supper seeing how many English peas she could mash into her ears.

She fingerpainted the dog with chocolate syrup and varnished the refrigerator front with molasses.

I often considered using a fire hose to clean the dining room after her meals.

And this is the young lady who, once on a hot summer day, stashed the last scoop of her double-dip chocolate ice cream cone in her pants pocket. She wanted to save it for later.

So, next time your baby presses her peanut butter sandwich through the screened door, next time she rubs mashed rutabaga into the air-conditioning vents and paints your white satin drapes with melted strawberry Jello, remember . . .

There is hope.

Six Thousand and Counting

In honor of Mother's Day, I decided to count up the days I've been a mother.

The total is so staggering, I'm going to spend the rest of the day recuperating in bed.

Eighteen years, times 365 days, plus the extra months and odd days since my firstborn arrived, comes to 6,622 days of nonstop motherhood.

I mention this only in order to establish my credentials. I am an Experienced Mother.

Unfortunately, experience doesn't count for much since each new day of motherhood brings astounding discoveries.

Mothers make more discoveries every day than Christopher Columbus made in a lifetime.

If I try hard, close my eyes and really concentrate, I can remember what it felt like not to be a mother. The last time I wasn't a mother, I was 24 and ever so naïve. It was an uncluttered, uncomplicated time.

Now I am vastly wiser, and on this Mother's Day, I would like to share with my young readers—those who aren't mothers yet—some of the discoveries one makes during 6,622 days of motherhood.

Listen, my children, and attend.

• When you're in the hospital following childbirth, the nurses periodically bring the baby to your room. It's just adorable, wrapped in its little blanket and cooing softly. Look at that fuzzy round head. Look at those big, blue eyes, that rosebud mouth. Oh, how sweet.

It's after you get baby home that you discover the truth about new babies: No one has told you that they can yell nonstop for hours no matter how much you feed them, rock them, walk them and croon inanities into their soft little ears. And no one has told you that a baby, for all its tiny size and limited diet, can make worse smells than all Farmer Brown's Poland China pigs.

Suddenly, you realize why the nurses smiled so happily as you and baby departed the maternity floor.

● Baby is 2. By this time, you've been spit up on, thrown up on, wet on and insulted in more odorous ways dozens of times. Now baby is toddling and has a full set of sharp little teeth. It's time for new discoveries.

Baby loves to pull things off tables—like your china and crystal—and watch them smash on the floor. Baby puts rows of little tooth marks on the coffee table, the piano and on you. Baby eats bugs. She uses the manicure scissors to style her hair and to trim the cat.

● Baby is 5, and you discover how adept she is with those little, dimpled hands. Baby finds daddy's tool box and saws off two of her bedposts one day during naptime. Baby removes the windshield wipers from your car and all the knobs from the television set. She fluff-dries the cat in the clothes dryer.

● Now she is 6. Baby goes to school, and you discover she isn't a genius after all. She hates homework, can't count and prints her letters backwards. At this point she's a tomboy—into tree-climbing and trampolines and is learning to ride a bicycle. You discover the emergency room and get to know its staff on a first-name basis.

● Baby is 8. She's freckle-faced, snaggle-toothed and she wants a pony. Her room is full of stuffed animals, and she brings home stray kittens.

One day she tells you she's built a tree house, and you're so proud—till you discover she's used the slats from her bed and the center leaf from your dining room table, all hammered into your best magnolia tree with ten-penny nails.

● Now she's 12, and she's discovered boys and the telephone. She giggles a lot. She experiments with makeup and wants a bikini. You spend your time keeping track of where she is and who she's with. One day you look in the mirror and discover your first gray hairs and fine lines around your eyes—a direct result of constant vigilance.

● She's 16 and drives too fast. She calls boys "men." You make the shattering discovery that she has a curvy figure. You regard all boys as The Enemy, wait up for her to come in at night, and you pray a lot. More gray hairs, and the lines aren't so fine anymore.

● She's 18, and she has a job. She buys her own clothes and makeup and still brings home stray kittens. She's going to college. She's in love, and she asks for a later curfew. You discover that you're a very nervous person.

One other thing they don't tell you about motherhood is that these 6,622 days pass very quickly. In retrospect, it's hard to believe how fast it's all happened.

At Home:
Life in the Spin Cycle
(Or, "Mom, It's a Jungle in There")

*Keeping house is like threading beads on a string with
no knot at the end.*

—anon.

When they finally get around to painting my portrait for the Working
Mother's Hall of Fame, I hope they caption it "The Madonna of the Mop."
I know a great deal about mopping and hold a Master of Mopping degree
(it's called a MOM) from the college of experience.

It isn't that I dislike housework, you understand, it's just that there are
other things I do better. Actually, I'm a whiz at mopping but, frankly, I'd
rather write. I guess that's why our house has always worn the look of a
house run by someone who'd rather be typing.

I Hate Superwomen

I have given up reading ladies' homemaking magazines. They give me an inferiority complex.

What really bothers me is the inevitable article about the Homemaker of the Year. This is always an attractive-looking lady with seven clean children and a proud-looking husband.

At the top of the page is a color picture of the happy family, standing in front of their home in the suburbs.

The stairstep children are in a neat row in the front of the picture, smiling like angels. If you look closely, you will notice that not a single one of them is pinching, kicking, stepping on the toes of, or otherwise harrassing the one standing next to him. Not a single one is sticking out his tongue or making a face at the camera. Not one is wiggling, squirming, pulling at his collar or scratching anywhere.

It's impossible. No one's children would all stand still long enough for a photographer to take that kind of picture without at least one of them doing one of those things.

Behind the children are the parents. The Homemaker of the Year has shiny, well-kept hair. The article tells you she does it herself. She never goes to the beauty parlor, preferring to save the money for family outings and fun. Her dress is tailored perfectly and is color-coordinated with the clothes of the children. The article tells you she makes all of the clothes her family wears, including her husband's shirts and ties, in her spare time. When she is not making their clothes, she makes the sheets, towels, afghans, bedspreads, curtains and drapes for the house.

Notice how proud and happy her husband looks. He is beaming at her fondly, wearing one of the shirts and ties she made in her spare time.

Down in the lefthand corner of the photo is the family dog. He has a shiny, silken coat. He is not scratching fleas or rolling in the dirt. He has not just been running through a field of beggar lice or burrs. He is not gnawing on the daily paper. The article tells you that each day the Homemaker of the Year takes time out from her household chores to brush and comb the dog and take him to obedience school.

She loves to cook. Subsequent photos show her in the kitchen, happily stirring the pot. Her children aren't hanging around saying, "But I'm hungry NOW." Instead, her children are in the dining room, setting the table. They are not fighting over who will put out the forks and who will put out the knives and who will fold the napkins. It seems her children never fight. In her spare time, she has taught them to share and to compromise.

The house is lovely. No handprints around the light switches. All the houseplants are green and thriving. No drooping stems or falling leaves with mysterious brown spots. Through the window, flowers can be seen blooming in the garden. She loves to garden and spends most of her spare time arranging flowers she has grown—that is, when she's not cooking, sewing, brushing the dog or teaching her children to share and to compromise.

The yard is neat and clean. She cuts the grass herself and keeps the trees and shrubs pruned. Money that would have been spent for a yardman goes into the kitty for family outings and fun. Nary a tree has two-by-fours nailed to it with ten-penny nails. Apparently her little boys have never discovered where dad keeps the hammer or the scrap lumber. No odd-looking structures of any kind have been constructed by her children anywhere in her yard. No bicycles, tricycles or toy trucks dot her driveway. Her children keep their toys inside the house, in toyboxes she built in her spare time.

Besides her homemaking chores (which aren't really chores at all—she vows that she loves every minute of it) she holds down a full-time executive position with a large advertising firm and does volunteer work at the local hospital. She is a Sunday School teacher, president of the garden club, chairman of the PTA fund-raising committee and chief organizer of a county humane society.

What is her secret? (And here comes the part that makes me sick.) She says:

"I make sure I get plenty of rest."

The Presence of My Anemones

Well, I've done it again.

Last year I planted all my bulbs in October.

They came up in November and froze in December.

So this year I decided to wait and plant them after Christmas.

This year I planted them in January.

They came up in February and froze in February.

It's discouraging not to have a green thumb.

I have a book called, "How to Grow Bulbs," which tells all about it from A to Z. On the front is a picture of a lady wearing gardening gloves and holding a trowel and a big bouquet of flowers she just grew.

She is also wearing a dressy dress, all her makeup, a big smile, and her hair looks like she just came home from the beauty parlor.

That is not how I look while gardening.

I am not a neat gardener. By the time I get through digging and planting, I look like an animated soil sample.

I garden with the how-to book in one hand to tell me what to do and a kitchen spoon in the other hand. Our trowel disappeared into the sandbox years ago and has never emerged again. And some mittenless moppet borrowed my gardening gloves during the big snow, and after the thaw only one reappeared.

What I like best to plant are anemones, or wind flowers. They are lovely, growing close to the ground with lacy little leaves. From a distance they resemble parsley. The blooms are white, pink, red or blue with some occasional purples, and they all have dark centers. They nod in the breeze and are altogether delightful little flowers.

I know this because I have see them blooming in other people's yards.

Please understand that anemones are not all that easy to plant. To begin with, they are not bulb-shaped bulbs like irises or tulips. Irises and tulip bulbs have definite tops and bottoms, so that even I can tell which end goes up.

Anemones are "tuberous rhizomes," according to the book, little brown lumps with bristles on one side. If the bristles are clearly visible, you place the lump bristle-side-down in the hole you have just dug with your kitchen spoon.

Unfortunately, the bristles are seldom clearly visible, so you have to decide which side of the lump looks like it might grow bristles later and plant that side down. Otherwise your flowers wll come up in China, as they say.

Actually, there was one year when, out of three packets of anemone bulbs, six came up and two actually bloomed. One was red and one was white.

They were beautiful, and my family was amazed.

So was I.

Anyone for Housework?

My children have been playing Monopoly.

I am considering inventing a game or two of my own. In fact, I have already made one up. It's called Housework.

Instead of a game board, you use a contemporary family-size house, complete with unmade beds, dirty dishes, bathtub rings and dusty furniture.

The first object of the game is to try to get anyone to play. This is difficult but not impossible. Methods include threats, bribery, blackmail, trickery and coercion. Under my rules, any of these is legal.

If none of the above is successful, however, the game may be played by one person. If you're playing it solitaire, you wait until no one else is at home and then you merrily whisk through the house, cleaning it all up yourself. This is the quickest method.

But if no one is going anywhere, you can make it a team game, dividing up as follows: The mother is one team. Everybody else in the family is the other team.

The object is for the mother to get the whole house clean before the other team can mess it up again.

As far as I know, no mother has ever won the game this way.

However, you can just play for points if you want to, as follows:

You win five points if you can cook and serve a hot meal—meat, at least two vegetables, bread, iced tea and dessert—and then get the whole kitchen cleaned up before someone comes in to make a peanut butter sandwich.

Three points if you get all the laundry done before any two children change clothes more than three times.

If you can find the scotch tape when you need it, give yourself two points.

Cleaning the ring out of the bathtub without disturbing the pet turtle is worth six points.

Matching up all the socks in the laundry without any left-over odd ones is a 10-point effort.

If the breakfast cereal you bought is the kind they wanted this week, add five points to your score.

And if your house is clean and straight with no newspapers on the floor, shoes in the middle of the room or toys in the chairs when Sunday afternoon company drops by, give yourself 250 points, pass "Go" and collect $250. You're ready for the national playoffs.

Let Me Entertain You

I know a lady who gives perfect dinner parties.

Her food is excellent, superbly complemented by the wine she selects. Her table is delightful. She arranges her own flowers, all cut from her garden and color-coordinated with the napkins and china.

Nary a speck of tarnish mars her silver, and her crystal is unspotted. Occasionally she goes in for the creative touch, serving dessert, for instance, in little tin pails tied with gingham bows.

Her children, shining cherubs in crisp, clean clothes, appear just long enough to delight her guests with their dainty manners. They lisp adorable pleasantries before disappearing sweetly into the nursery for the rest of the evening.

All this is a perfection that I'm going to achieve someday. In the meantime, I am learning to cope.

In my spotty career on the entertainment front, I have given a few dinner parties. None has been perfect, and several are replayed occasionally in my nightmares.

In defense, I have developed a certain fatalism. After many years of organizing dinner parties, I have come to expect—and try to plan for—one or more nerve-shattering occurrences:

As the hot, sultry day of the party dawns, the air conditioner will groan and die, leaving me a span of about eight hours to hunt up a repairman. For this reason, I try never to entertain on Saturdays, Sundays or holidays, when repairmen are hard to find. In the meantime, with the house growing hotter and steamier by the minute, the candles on the table melt, reshaping themselves in tired curves. It's a good idea always to keep an extra set of candles in the freezer.

Of course, if the party is held in the depths of winter, it's the furnace that quits. Once I compensated for this by lighting a fire in the fireplace, only to remember too late that the flue was closed. People in their best evening finery, groping through a murky cloud of smoke, are not happy dinner guests.

These are the reasons that I now entertain only in the spring and the fall.

In any season, the oven, the ice maker, the vacuum cleaner or the plumbing can give up the ghost, and probably will—particularly if I've invited people I'm trying to impress. Consequently, I never invite people I am trying to impress. If you are invited for dinner at my house, know that I consider you a close and understanding friend.

An hour before the party begins, at least two children will begin running fever. One will develop the throw-ups and other dire symptoms that suggest cholera or plague. The other child will break out in large red spots resembling measles, smallpox or acute allergy. I've found it handy always to include a doctor on my guest list.

The remaining child will have forgotten all about my party and will have invited her entire class over for a rock fest in the playroom. Once she invited her Latin class for a toga party, and my guests were startled when a horde of teen-age Romans joined them in the buffet line, all wearing sheets and laurels of honeysuckle in their hair.

During the party, the cat will have kittens, usually on the coats my guests have put on my bed. Now, if the cat is pregnant, I suspend dinner parties for the duration or else invite a veterinarian and hang up the guests' coats.

After weeks of blooming in lovely profusion, the flowers in my garden go into their annual dormant period just in time not to bloom for a centerpiece. The few that are blooming on the day of the party harbor lots of little bugs that wait until my guests are seated, then come out and crawl around inquisitively on the tablecloth.

But while I am waiting to evolve into the perfect hostess, I am comforted by one fact. I never have to worry about the ultimate horror that every other hostess fears—that her guests, usually delightful conversationalists, will sit around stolidly like so many manikins, unable to think of anything to say to each other.

At my parties, everyone is so busy coping with crises that conversation just flows naturally. Birthing kittens, teens in togas, mysterious diseases, smoking fireplaces, buggy flowers and dying appliances are excellent ice breakers.

House for Sale

Our house is for sale. I mention this just in case any of you out there is interested in purchasing a 4 bedroom res. complete with den, playrm, pool and dbl. carport. Large yd. Excel. condition, of course. Inhabited by little old lady, her three children and four cats. House is neat. It has taken us more than a month to get it that way.

Selling your house is a lot like having a big party. You have to clean everything up and make it look as if you live that way all the time.

The only difference is that a party happens all at once, and then it ends. Afterwards you can collapse among the dirty dishes, secure in the knowledge that things will get back to normal in the morning, and you won't have to do it again for awhile.

But when you're selling a house, not only do you have to clean it up, you have to keep it that way. Day after day. Clean enough for people to see. Clean enough for people to want. It's nerve-shattering.

All this cleanliness has considerably altered our lifestyle. And I made some mistakes.

For example, one of the first things I did, about a month ago, in preparation for showing the house was to clean the oven. Once it was clean, I dared anyone to use it. Now we are dining on things you don't have to cook, unless they can be cooked on the outdoor grill. I feel a little silly scrambling eggs in the back yard each morning, but . . .

Another mistake was to clean the fireplace the same day. As soon as I did, the thermometer plummeted to sub-freezing readings. Did we have a fire? Yes, we did. Are the remains of the fire—ashes and such—still lurking in the fireplace now? Yes, they are. So, this weekend, I get to clean the fireplace again. Whee.

Having folks drop in at all hours to look at the house has taught me the secrets of the instant cleanup. You'd be surprised what you can do in that little interval between the time the doorbell rings and the moment when you open the door.

Did you know that in the space of 60 seconds it's possible to: take out the trash, toss the cats into the clothes dryer, slip their food dish into the refrigerator and sweep the mail and last Sunday's paper into a dresser drawer?

Well, it is. And you still have time to remove an entire science project on ants from the dining room table (a fire ant display in jars looks innocent among the cans in the kitchen cabinet). Then you can open the front door, serenely, of course, as if you had merely been sitting around reading a book.

But I fear I am becoming like Pavlov's dog. When my phone rang last week at the office, I cleared everything from my desk top into the top drawer in three seconds flat before I remembered I wasn't at home.

But this whole experience has made me really proud of my children. They have exhibited unprecedented neatness.

I praised my eldest recently—usually the messiest one of all—for the way she has her bed made each morning as soon as she gets up.

"It's easy," she said. "I just sleep on top of the bedspread."

The middle child has also become a model of cleanliness. No dirty jeans dangle from her light fixture. No wet towels are draped over her bedposts. This week I discovered why. Every morning on the way to school, she deposits her dirty laundry in the trunk of the car.

Having your house on the market has a lot of advantages. I'll think of some in a minute. For one thing, while you're cleaning up, you find a lot of things you've lost over the years.

While raking out the carport, I found a box of items that have been missing since we moved into the house two years ago. It contained a pair of still-in-the-box, never-worn, sparkling-white, size 7 sneakers that I bought for my son and misplaced before he ever wore them (today he wears a size 10); also the top to the blender I gave away last month because I couldn't find its top and a library book that was due back on Sept. 27, 1979. I also unearthed a sack of petrified oranges.

My only consolation is that, somewhere out there, there is someone else who is going through the same ordeal. When I buy her house, I hope she's cleaned the fireplace and the oven.

Six Legs
Is Two Legs Too Many

My son was amused. "Mom, it's just a little roach," he said, stepping squishily on the offender. He scraped up the mashed remains with a paper napkin and deposited them in the trash. Ick.

"You can come down now," he told me.

I was standing on a chair (that's where I always stand when there's a roach in the room). I was making shrill, incoherent noises and waving my arms around my head. Every shred of my dignity had flown out the window (that's where my dignity always flies when there's a roach in the room).

I have never seen a roach that was less than four feet long. A friend of mine refers to all roaches as attack roaches—an excellent description.

I have (on more than one occasion) stood on a straight chair for an hour or more, waiting for someone to come home and rescue me from an attacking roach.

Usually by the time someone arrives, the roach has long since returned through the wall to wherever roaches go; and there I stand, on my chair in the roachless room, looking stupid.

There are people who are afraid of small, enclosed spaces; others are afraid of the great outdoors. Some folks are afraid of cats (I'll never understand this), and some folks are afraid of thunder.

I am afraid of anything that has more than four legs—crawly spiders and bugs, roaches in particular.

Bring on your uncaged elephants, your lions and hippopotami, and I remain unperturbed.

Bring on your snakes, and I remain calm (relatively); your lizards and crawfish I can observe with a detached eye. Mice are cute, as long as they keep their distance, and chipmunks are adorable, even gnawing in my garden.

But roaches trip my alarm. The only good roach is a dead one, and even dead ones are pretty terrible.

Our new house came equipped with battalions of roaches, rivaling the populations of, say, New York or Chicago. Several times in recent weeks I have called the pest control people to come out and control my pests. They have sprayed diligently in, around and under the house, and still the roaches flourish.

We didn't have any roaches at our old house, and now I know why. They were all at the new house, busily training their armies and waiting for me to arrive.

While cooking supper on this particular occasion, I had opened a cabinet door to get the syrup when I came face to face with one of the patriarchs of the clan. Fully armed, he was crouched between a can of soup and the catfood. (I will not discuss here how the soup, the syrup and the catfood came to be in the same cabinet. Yes, it's a commentary on my housekeeping, but it's irrelevant.)

This roach was one of the shiny, black, jumbo jet variety. (Roaches come in three species: shiny black jumbo jet, mottled brown battle cruiser and the slightly smaller, rust colored armored tank with wings.)

This roach bared its teeth and growled horribly before charging over the edge of the shelf and diving with a kamikaze whine toward my feet. As it was on its way down, I was on my way up—into the nearest chair, where I hopped up and down screaming while our pancakes burned.

Roaches have an advantage over people: With six legs, they can move much faster than we can. And they are very hostile.

When they aren't busy attacking you from cabinets or closets, they enjoy lying around in corners on their backs, as if dead. Then, when you gather your courage to approach with the broom, they wave their dreadful, hairy feet, signaling their comrades to come out and attack.

Another favorite war game is a version of the old Chinese torture trick. A roach will crawl across the ceiling while you're lying in bed and hang there, eight feet up, directly over your face. He'll walk around patiently in tiny circles, waiting for you to open your mouth. After 10 nerve-wracked minutes of straining your eyes in the dark and yawning with your mouth shut, you move to another room. A roach can hang on your bedroom ceiling for a week of nights, while you toss and turn on the lumpy living room couch. And whenever you manage to go to sleep you have a recurring nightmare in which you forget and yawn with your mouth open.

They say that roaches roamed the earth long before mankind did and that their armies will be here long after we're gone. I don't understand this. Roaches are so revolting, how can they stand each other long enough to procreate?

Daisy, Daisy

One of the pleasures of moving into a home is discovering the plants that emerge in the flower beds in the spring.

Since you don't know what to expect, it's a happy surprise when a row of bulbs suddenly appears or a clump of daylilies sends long narrow leaves pushing up out of a bare spot in the soil.

But I've learned the hard way that it pays to know what you're growing.

Take, for instance, the discovery I made early this year in a backyard flower bed. While weeding, I noticed a flat circle of leaves nestled in the pine straw behind some iris. "Aha!" I thought gleefully. "A Gerbera daisy."

Mentally, I blessed the former tenant who had left me a Gerbera. I have raised more Gerbera daisy leaves than the average gardener, but nary a Gerbera has ever bloomed for me. I have seen them blooming profusely in other people's yards, sending up tall stems topped by rosy pink, coral or dusty yellow blossoms.

Now, I thought, I have a well-established, though apparently neglected, daisy. I decided to transplant it into my new flower bed in which I had worked diligently. The soil was dark, rich and well-turned, and I had dug in lots of fertilizer last fall. It seemed a perfect spot for a Gerbera to flourish and bloom.

Contrary to usual plant behavior, the Gerbera didn't even wilt after being transplanted. I watered it carefully and was delighted after a few days when it rewarded me with some new leaves and bright green shoots. It was obviously very happy.

Proudly, I pointed it out to visitors. It basked in the attention, unfurling new leaves almost daily. I fertilized it, watered it, nurtured it and talked to it, and it responded with more and more leaves.

In the meantime, daffodils I had planted sprang up around the Gerbera and for several weeks took the spotlight as their creamy blossoms nodded in the spring breezes.

Now and then, I would notice the Gerbera, tucked snugly behind the daffodils, growing swiftly. I marveled that I had never seen one quite so sturdy.

During two busy weeks at the office, I failed to do much gardening. Imagine my surprise on a sunny Saturday morning when I went out to the flower bed and found that the Gerbera was almost two feet tall, overshadowing the daylilies which were just getting a good start, and thick with heavy, new green leaves.

A tiny doubt troubled the back of my mind. Could it be that this wasn't a Gerbera after all? Nonsense, I told myself. It looked just like a Gerbera a few weeks ago. But, said the tiny doubt, Gerberas are low, compact plants. This plant was big and bushy, resembling a rangy cabbage that refused to head up.

It grew like Jack's beanstalk. It looked less and less like a Gerbera and more like, well, maybe a tobacco plant. It was huge and scruffy looking. It dominated the garden, looming over the other plants that were minding their business and growing daintily as garden plants should.

When it reached three feet in height, throwing deep shadows over the phlox and baby hollyhocks, I finally gave in to the doubt, which had grown as big as the plant.

I wasn't raising a Gerbera. I was harboring an imposter, a robust renegade whose tap root was probably somewhere in China by now. I thought of all the fertilizer I had given it, the time I had spent carefully transplanting it, watering it, even talking to it, for Pete's sake! I was furious. I had been outsmarted by a weed. That's a stupid feeling.

The obvious solution was to get the shovel, dig the intruder up and throw it on the compost heap.

I got the shovel and with immense resolve headed toward the garden where the weed sat sunning itself and probably feasting on fertilizer that very minute.

I dug it up and threw it on the compost heap. It occurred to me that the weed looked sort of sad, lying on its side with its roots drying in the sunshine. My conscience pricked me. After all, I was the one who had treated it kindly, given it a home, so to speak, and encouraged it to grow. It really couldn't help being a weed.

I worked in the flower bed through most of the afternoon and considered what to plant in the bare space where the weed had flourished. Nothing came to mind.

That night I couldn't sleep. Thoughts of the poor weed wilting on the compost heap kept bothering me. After all, it had done its best.

The next day I went out and replanted the weed in the garden.

It has grown a foot taller and has sprouted more new leaves. Whatever it is, I must be the only person in Macon who is growing one on purpose. I've decided to call it a Mystery Plant.

Kids Grow,
But They Don't Forget Laundry Games

Last weekend the children arranged to be out when it was time to do the laundry. I wound up doing all of it, and whatever we weren't wearing got washed. It was a long weekend.

It's been several years since I did all the laundry. Ages ago—as soon as I had determined that the members of my little tribe had grown tall enough to reach the washer and dryer control knobs—I resigned as wash lady for the multitudes.

"It's time for you people to do your own laundry," I told them and conducted lessons in washer and dryer operation.

I also gave tips about not washing white things with colored things. After a couple of weeks wearing pink underwear, they learned.

For a while, life was hunky dory. I did have a problem with my son who discovered with glee that if you dump in an extra cupful of soap, you get a fascinating pile of suds oozing down the sides of the washer, across the floor, out the door and into the kitchen.

But for the most part, things went well. The trick is to teach kids how to run household machinery while they're small and think it's a lark. They love turning the knobs and hearing those big machines hum. It makes them feel powerful.

It's only when they're old enough to realize it's a drag that they—well, realize it's a drag. By then, you've escaped countless hours in front of the washer and dryer and behind the vacuum cleaner. You can pour yourself a glass of iced tea, prop your feet on the coffee table and read a magazine while the household chugs along.

But lately my crowd has discovered that life holds more interesting pastimes than washing and vacuuming. Now it's a battle of wits to see who does the laundry. And last weekend I lost the battle.

I also discovered while gathering dirty clothes from odd places that my children are still playing the games they played years ago. If you've ever done the family laundry, you may recognize one or two:

Wad and Toss: This game is usually played in the bedroom or bathroom prior to taking a shower. You undress, shut your eyes, wad up your clothes and toss them into the air. If they dangle from a ceiling fixture you get 10 points. If they merely fall to the floor, kick them under the bed and give yourself five points. If they land in that little space between the back of the hamper and the wall, you get 25 points. No points if they land in the hamper.

My son sometimes plays Wad and Toss in the utility room. He undresses there, takes time for a quick game of Wad and Toss and wears a towel to the bathroom for his shower. In the utility room, you get 30 points if the clothes land in the little space between the back of the washer and the wall. You also get to watch, from time to time, as your agile mom climbs up on top of the washer and tries to fish them out with an unbent coat hanger. But be prepared to run when she discovers they are yours.

Banana Peel: Another pre-shower activity. Grasp your jeans and underwear firmly at the waistband and peel them off in one swift motion, turning the jeans wrong-side-out with the undies caught neatly in the pants legs. If you're really proficient, you can catch the tops of your socks on the way down and capture them in two neat little balls inside the jeans legs. This all-in-one motion is quicker than taking things off one at a time. It's also more fun. Now you're ready to play Wad and Toss with the whole thing.

Hide-and-Go-Sock: Take your socks off. Throw one of them onto the back of your top closet shelf. Leave the other one on the floor, or use it for a round of Wad and Toss. In a few weeks, half of your socks will be in the closet, and your mom will be grumbling about not being able to match up your socks. Before long, she'll go out and buy you some new ones. She'll keep the odd socks for a long time, hoping their mates will show up. But one day she'll get tired of looking at all those odd socks, and she'll throw them away or make dolls out of them. As soon as she does this, clean out the top of your closet and put all the hidden socks in the laundry. This will drive your mother batty.

The games go on and on. Swap: leave all your clothes at camp and bring home those of your cabin mate who is two sizes smaller than you and lives in Anchorage. Confetti: leave a few Kleenex in your shirt pocket as it goes into the washer. Tie/Dye: tie knots in the arms of your new white button-down. Wash it with your new jeans.

There are fun games to be played with the vacuum cleaner, too. But I've run out of space.

Single Parenting

When the children were not yet teen-agers, their father and I went our separate ways, and I became a single parent.

Single parenting is a mixed bag. One day the bag is filled with hassles; the next, it's full of fun. And raising teens alone is a trick-or-treat proposition—you never know what's coming, so you'd better be ready for anything.

A single-parent family becomes a working unit—not always a smoothly functioning working unit, but a working unit just the same. There's a great deal of learning and of shared responsibility. And there's a great deal of love.

And there are also plenty of those situations in which you tell yourself, "Someday I'll laugh about this."

Where There's a Will . . .

This week I feel very efficient, having done one of those things about which people often procrastinate—one of those things about which I have procrastinated for the past five years and a few months.

I have had a will drawn. Now I can go to my final reward secure in the knowledge that my vast holdings (including my cents-off grocery store coupons and my $6.32 savings account) will be disposed of according to my wishes.

At least I guess they will. Since learning of my project, the children have become intensely interested in how things are to be divided. They have also redesigned my plans.

Because they are the heirs to my estate (I love that word; it sounds so grand and important), I thought they should know what I was up to.

My son was handy, so I told him about it first. His eyes brightened at the prospect.

"You mean we get to own the house?"

I tried to explain about mortgages. He brushed that aside, intent on more important matters.

"After you're dead, can I paint my room black and have a strobe light?"

I assured him that the decor of his room would be a matter of little importance to me following my demise.

Then he thought of something even more tantalizing.

"Do we get to own the cars?" He has just turned 15. Cars have taken on immense importance in his life.

I tried to explain about car payments. His enthusiasm was undampened. "Wow," he said. "That'll be neat."

He fetched his sisters and brought them to my room. I heard them coming down the hall with him in the lead, explaining brightly along the way that I had arranged for the three of them to own everything.

" . . . and as soon as Mom dies, we get the cars," he was chattering as they entered the room. He is apparently under the impression that I am planning to meet my end in the immediate future.

The girls were somewhat more tactful in their approach, but not much.

"Why are you drawing a will?" asked the elder one. "Gee, Mom, don't you feel well?"

Touched by this intimation of affection, I explained that the drawing of a will is simply an essential part of a well-planned financial program.

They were more interested in the particulars of the three-way split.

"Who gets the cats?" they wanted to know.

"Can I have your hair curlers?"

"Can we throw out your plants or do we have to keep watering them?"

"Hey, we can have a yard sale with all your junk. If we sell your arrow-head collection, how much is it worth?"

"How do we get your money out of the bank?"

"If there are only two cars and there are three of us, how do we divide them up?" This from my son. His mind is a one-way street.

"I want the television."

"I get the stereo."

My middle child went to my jewelry box and peered inside. Her face grew long. "Not much here," she commented.

"But just think," said the eldest. "All the phones will be ours."

"And the phone bills, too," I cautioned.

And so it has continued. The subject of their inheritance has been the favored topic of dinner table conversation for a week. I have begun to feel acutely mortal.

Shortly after we went to bed one night recently, my son tiptoed to my bedside in the dark.

"Mom?"

"Ummm?"

"You still alive?"

"Afraid so."

"I was just thinking. If you went ahead and bought another car now, you could put it in your will, and then we'd each get one."

Refrigerator Literature

If archaeologists in, say, the year 3000 want a chronicle of American family life in the 1980s, I hope they dig up our refrigerator. It tells the story of the day-to-day life of a family of four in which three children go to two schools at two different times of day, and the mother works full time.

Our household revolves around our refrigerator message center. The refrigerator front is laden with little notes—things we forgot to tell each other last time our paths crossed.

The notes are usually written to each other, but my son also writes reminders to himself.

Since no one's ever sure which of the notes is still viable, they are rarely removed, just covered up under deepening layers of newer notes. A lot of the notes are answers to other notes, and taken all together, they tell little family stories.

Last week I went looking for the refrigerator and couldn't find it. It had disappeared under two years worth of notes, all stuck on with little refrigerator-note magnets. We have so many little magnets that you can't use a compass within a two-mile radius of our house.

I cleaned off the notes and was amazed to discover that our refrigerator is painted green. Somehow, in the days since I last saw it, I had forgotten that.

Here is a sampling of what I removed last week, freeing countless little magnets for new duty:

*   *   *

"H: When you get home from school today, please pull up the dandelions in the backyard and plant the five little azalea bushes. Mom."

"H: Pull dandelions. Plant ezalias. H."

*   *   *

"(7 a.m.) To Whom it May Concern: I lost a green contact lens in my carpet near my closet. Whoever finds it gets a quarter. N."

"(8 a.m.) N: I found your contact. When I get the quarter, you can have it. H."

"(3 p.m.) H: Here is your quarter. Thanks. N." (Rough spot on note showed where quarter had been taped.)

"(4 p.m.) Mom: I'm at Sam's. Can I have some lunch money tomorrow? I've only got a quarter. H."

"(6 p.m.) H: What did you do with the money I gave you yesterday? I'm going to the grocery store. See you later. Mom."

*   *   *

"The things in the dishwasher are clean. This is a public service announcement."

*   *   *

"Everybody: I am on a diet. The fruit and vegetables in the humidrawer are mine. I paid for them. I also counted them. Don't eat them. N."

*   *   *

"Mom: My class ring has arrived. Please leave me $100 this afternoon so I can go pick it up. N."

"N: I thought the ring wasn't going to be ready till next month. You can get your ring, or we can eat for the next two weeks. Take your pick. Mom."

"Mom: I pick the ring. N."

*   *   *

"Anybody: I need to borrow $5 till allowance day. S."

"S: I'll lend you $5 if you'll pay me back $6. H."

"S: You still owe me $5 from last time. Mom."

"S: I'll lend you $5 if you'll let me wear your pink shirt tomorrow. N."

"N: Put the money on my bed, and I'll leave the shirt in your closet. Thanks. S."

*   *   *

"(5 p.m.) Mom: Some guy named Phil or Bill said he's got to talk to you before tomorrow. It's very important. Call him. I've gone out to ride my bike. H."

"(6 p.m.) H: I know three Bills and two Phils. Do you have any more clues? I'm going to the grocery store. Mom."

"(7:30 p.m.) Mom: All I know is he had a sort of medium-deep voice. Does that help? I've gone to the picture show. H."

*   *   *

"(Mon.) Mom: There is a gray kitten in the tree outside my window. He's cute. Can we keep him? S."

"S: No way. Mom."

"(Tues.) Mom: I got the kitten to come down out of the tree. I shut him in your bathroom with some food. Can't we keep him? He's so cute. S."

"S: No way. I put him back outside. Mom."

"(Wed.) Mom: He was still here, so I fed him again. He has such cute little eyes. If we can keep him, I'll take care of him. Please? S."

"S: Here is a check and a grocery list. I guess you'd better get some kitten food, too. He does have cute eyes, doesn't he? Mom."

Staying in Touch

The gentleman has two sons in their late teens. They stand up when I enter the room. They say "Yes, Ma'am" to me, hold the door for me and compliment my dress.

They're nice young men, confident, friendly, outgoing. I see them on weekends when they are home from the university, busy with their cars and dates and the things that interest teen-age boys. I wonder if my own children are as secure and happy as those two seem to be.

Often they invite their dad to accompany them on Saturday afternoon fishing expeditions. He goes. The trips result in fried fish suppers, concocted with lots of cornmeal and conversation by three males in the kitchen.

A good bit of noisy joking and kidding around accompanies this activity, interspersed with serious talk of something called "wrapping flies," which is apparently a fascinating rainy day pastime for fishing enthusiasts.

He is also invited to help them tinker on their two automobiles. He does. Three pairs of ankles and feet are the only visible parts of them as they lie under the cars, working and talking of cables, cam shafts and universal joints.

He invites them to help him with the yard work. They accept. They kid him about his old lawnmower. He's crazy about his old lawnmower. They tell him that when he dies, they'll erect it over his grave instead of a tombstone. They all laugh. It's an old family joke.

Yard work, like fishing and automobile tuning, is a family affair with these three.

He has raised them alone since they were toddlers. Well, not really alone. He had an excellent housekeeper for many years who saw to meals, laundry and the things that go into the keeping of a household. I think she threw a lot of mothering and homemade cookies into the bargain.

He says he doesn't understand how I work full time and raise three teenagers without a housekeeper. I tell him it's easy—the housework doesn't get done. He laughs.

I tell him I don't understand how he has managed to maintain such a close relationship with his sons. His work requires that he travel a lot. It always has. For many weeks of the boys' lives, he hasn't been home at all.

He laughs and tells me their phone bill for years rivaled the national debt as he called from various places around the world to check on the home front. He tells me that once he flew home from California to attend a kindergarten graduation, then flew back to his meeting the following day. I laugh.

"If I spent that much time away from my children, I'd lose touch with them," I tell him. He turns serious.

"You really wouldn't," he says. "It's a matter of caring more than mere physical presence."

I turn serious; I don't agree. There has to be lots of time together.

"No," he says, opening a can of beer and waving it around emphatically (he's very emphatic when he thinks he's right, which is usually). "There doesn't have to be lots of time. That's not the most important thing."

"Just what," I ask him, "is the most important thing?"

"Look," he says, stabbing the air with his beer can. "If I'm going to do the work that makes my life meaningful for me, I have to spend a lot of time away from home. That's the life I chose before their mother died.

"But they know I love them. They always know where I am, where they can reach me. I'll interrupt a meeting, miss a client and lose a sale to talk to them if they need me. When I'm home and they're home, we get together; we catch up on all the things that have happened."

"But is that enough?" I ask.

"It has to be enough," he says. "That's just the way it is. Who knows how much is enough anyway? You spend more time with your kids than I do with mine, and still you worry whether you're spending enough time with them. Parents who stay home all the time—mothers who don't work, fathers who don't travel—worry whether they're spending enough time."

I ponder this in silence. He's right, but I'm not sure that makes me wrong. I still think you have to spend a lot of time together.

"Look," he says, reinforcing his point, "the big question is, do you enjoy the time you spend with your kids?

"Do you want to be with them, talk with them, know what's important to them and what's going on in their lives?

"Because if you don't, then no amount of time you spend with them is going to make any difference.

"If you do, and they know it, then everything's OK. They don't need you with them all the time. They just need to know you want to be with them when you can.

"That's the important thing."

He's right, I know, as far as his argument goes. Still, I wouldn't want to spend weeks away from my children, so I don't think I'm completely wrong.

"I still think . . . ," I begin.

"I know what you think, but you're wrong," he says. He's grinning now; he knows I've run out of arguments. But then he looks a little uncertain. "At least, I hope you're wrong," he says.

So he's not sure either.

A Well Run House

The young man stopped his lawnmower and wiped his forehead on the towel he was wearing around his neck. His brother was carrying an arm-load of brush toward the curb.

"Your dad's lucky to have two such good yard keepers," I remarked by way of greeting.

They grinned. "Dad's in the kitchen. He said to tell you to just come on in when you got here," said one. "The doorbell's broken."

It was not without a degree of curiosity that I walked in and glanced around this bastion of bachelorhood. Very neat, I thought. Everything in place as usual.

This was the home of the man whose sons have come to spend the sum-mer with him. Several weeks ago, I predicted that two teen-age boys would wreak havoc in his usually pristine household.

"Never happen," was his response. "If they're going to live here, they're going to be neat."

My response to that was something to the effect of, "Hah!"

So, I couldn't help looking around as I walked toward the kitchen, and I was surprised to see that everything was neatness as usual.

I found my host arranging slices of pineapple around strawberries and bunches of green grapes on a plate.

"Very artistic," I said.

"Yes, it does look nice, doesn't it?" he replied, standing back and ad-miring his handiwork. He's a very confident person.

"And everything looks very clean and neat," I conceded, noting that there was even an arrangement of daylilies on the table, which was set for four. "I don't see how you do it with teens in the house."

"Nothing to it," he responded, grinning. "You just have to crack the whip, make sure they know who's boss."

"No, really, I want to know how you do it," I said, watching him re-move a bubbly casserole from the oven. "Maybe I should take lessons."

He looked very pleased. "It's easy. Every morning each one of them has to clean up his room and do his own laundry before anything else. I'm in charge of menus and meals and kitchen cleanup, and they each have a list of things they have to see about each day—clean the bathroom, take out the trash, dust, vacuum—you know, the usual stuff.

"It's simple," he said. "You would do well to follow my example."

I had to admit to a certain amount of admiration, never having had much success with the "simple" task of getting teens to do chores. Maybe I should initiate such a program at home, I thought. It certainly seems to work well here.

While he removed pork chops from the backyard grill, my job was to call the boys inside for supper and to tell them to be sure and wash their hands. These things accomplished, we all sat down to eat.

"This looks great, Dad," said the older of the two, stacking three pork chops on his plate and digging into the casserole.

"Yeah, this is good," remarked his younger brother, turning to me and adding conversationally, "Usually we just have tomato sandwiches."

Oh? I seized upon this bit of interesting information and said innocently, "Why, as much as your dad likes to cook, I thought you'd be eating like this three times a day."

Both boys laughed. "Dad's favorite recipe is microwaved pork and beans," continued the younger one. "He serves them on top of scrambled eggs. Yesterday we had them for lunch and for supper, too."

"How fascinating," I said. Their dad looked uncomfortable. "Eat your supper, son," he said.

A brief silence ensued, and the boys helped themselves to more of everything. "Are we having dessert?" asked the elder one. "I thought I saw some ice cream in the freezer."

"Yes," replied the father. "I did get some ice cream."

"Wow," said the younger. "We never have dessert. It's pretty neat having company. Except we had to clean up all day."

"Really," I asked. "How interesting. I thought it looked this way all the time."

The boys looked at each other and laughed and laughed. "You should have seen this place this morning," said the younger, whom I was beginning to regard as my informant. "It was a zoo. Dad hadn't washed the dishes in a week."

I glanced inquiringly at their father, who was wearing a peculiar look. "Son," he said, "eat your supper.

"Kids talk too much," he added. "And I bet you're going to write a column about this."

Now, would I do a thing like that?

A Responsible Kid

"Wow! It's the neatest car, Mom, really. Wait till you see. And it's time I got a car, you know? I mean, I'm 17 and I've got a good job, and my grades are OK. And I can handle a $1,500 loan. Mom, I know I can. I've always been a responsible kid.

"Can I buy the car?"

His eager eyes search my face, looking for a sign of acquiescence.

"I'm thinking," I tell him, and I am. But not really about the purchase of an automobile. The phrase "responsible kid" has triggered those questions that creep around in the backs of working mothers' minds, surfacing at times like this.

What sort of life has this been that made him so responsible? What is it like, being a responsible kid? What has he missed? Independence is a good thing, but has there been too much? Have I spent enough of what they call "quality time" with him?

He was 9 the long-ago day he stood looking up at me (he was a lot shorter then) as I talked on the kitchen telephone to the managing editor of this newspaper. I covered the mouthpiece with my hand and mouthed, "I got the job," and his face lit up as he ran to tell his sisters. Whether or not I got the job was important to them—it would determine where and how they lived.

We moved to a new town, I began working, and, at ages 12, 11 and 9, they entered a new world—the world of responsible kids.

Teachers became accustomed to notes from me, little memos outlining my peripatetic path for the day. ("I'll be in Alamo this morning, in Eastman after lunch. If you need me I can be reached at . . . "). Please help me take care of my child.

Neighbors got phone calls. ("There's been a bank robbery, and I have to go. Can he ride with you to Scouts?")

I got phone calls. ("Mom, I rode my bike home from school early. I've got a sore throat. You don't need to come. I took two aspirin.")

When their friends were out playing after school, my kids were sorting the light laundry from the dark and dialing the washer for gentle cycle.

Their classmates went home to a cheery greeting and homebaked cookies. My kids came home to notes on the refrigerator door. ("Look in the freezer and get out the container marked 'spaghetti' for supper. If you want a snack, there's Jello in the refrigerator.")

They mastered the microwave and got to know the town's repairmen. ("Mom, the dryer's not heating, so I called Mr. Smith.")

They learned to communicate with an absentee mother through secretaries ("Tell Mom I'm playing at Josh's house") and through notes ("Mom, I'm at the football field. I'll get a ride home").

They learned to cook, starting with hot dogs and progressing through cake-mix muffins to easy casseroles. With the telephone receiver tucked between ear and shoulder, they tackled beef stew ("Mom, what do I do after the onions get brown? Do I put in the tomatoes yet? Yes, but how much pepper?").

Late nights found me in their rooms, touching small, sleepy faces, assessing the emotional well-being, taking the inner temperature. "How was your day, fella? Did everything go OK? Tell me what happened."

The self-reliance, the unfailing optimism was humbling ("The bathroom light's out, Mom. I'll get some new lightbulbs on my way home from school tomorrow. I can change it easy").

At 16, with drivers' licenses, they ran errands ("Please pick up the dry cleaning before 5") and learned to grocery shop ("Mom, I got one of those roasts with the bone that looks like a 7. Is that OK?").

And eventually they got jobs of their own ("I'll be late getting home tonight, Mom. We have to unload the truck").

A working mother wonders many things. Are they all right? Are they alone too much? Are they happy? Random measurements are all she has to work with. He says, "Wow, Mom, my science project is really neat!" and she reads the tone, the enthusiasm, and worries less. His skies are sunny, and all's right with his world.

"I've always been a responsible kid, Mom," he says, looking earnest.

Can he handle a loan? Who am I to say no?

Back to Normal

Remember the days of the old-fashioned family—a father who worked, a mother who stayed at home and two or three children?

The people who keep track of social trends tell us that with so many women entering the working world such families have become a rarity.

Apparently so. After one of my daughters spent a week visiting in a traditional home, she looked as puzzled as if she'd been to Mars.

"It was strange, Mom. I haven't been in a house like that in years," she told me. "They sat around and talked, like on 'Father Knows Best,' and the whole house was clean all the time.

"And we didn't eat a single frozen dinner all week."

Right away I could tell this was going to be a depressing conversation.

"They don't even have a microwave," she went on. "Cindy's mom cooks on a regular stove. She even wears an apron."

In order to understand my daughter's perspective, you have to realize that for much of her life she has lived in a household where the homemaker is usually at the office. Our meals are planned about 20 minutes before they hit the table.

With wonder in her eyes, she related the unfamiliar situations encountered while on her visit.

"Cindy's mom is neat," she said. "You get the feeling that someone's really in charge of things around the house, someone is there all the time and has it all under control.

"It's not like around here. The whole family has chores to do, just like we do, but Cindy's mom does most of the housework. She even *likes* housework. And she keeps everything on a schedule.

"Everybody eats together," she related, shaking her head in near disbelief. "I felt like I was in 'The Brady Bunch.' Cindy's mom gets up each morning and fixes breakfast. Bacon, eggs, even biscuits. We had *milk*, Mom, glasses of milk at each place, along with our orange juice. Cindy's mom is big into nutrition.

"And get this," she burbled along, not noticing my lengthening face. "Cindy's mom has a little silver bell she rings when meals are ready, and nobody, *nobody*, can eat a bite until everybody is at the table. With clean hands.

"And they *never* go to Hardee's. We didn't eat in the car all week, not even once.

"And they have supper every night at 6:30 because that's when Cindy's dad gets home from the office. He's real nice. He's funny and cracks lots of jokes. It's strange, though, having a man in the house. You can't run around in your underwear."

But a man around the house is useful, she discovered.

"Cindy's dad opens the ketchup when the top is stuck. When company comes he fixes the drinks, and he is always the one who cuts the grass. Cindy doesn't even *know* how to start the lawnmower, and neither does her brother."

Cindy's dad also takes care of the family automobiles, she related.

"At the gas station, Cindy just gets the car filled up. She doesn't have the oil or the tires checked or anything. Her dad does all that on the weekend."

Another feature of this unusual household, she said, was the use of a tablecloth on the dinner table instead of plastic place mats. And no paper napkins.

"Real napkins made out of real cloth," she said. "Cindy's mom *irons* them. Imagine! And she does all the laundry for the whole family without shrinking anyone's sweaters in the dryer."

(That was a low blow. How did I know that sweater would shrink? My gloom increased.)

Obliviously, she bubbled along. "And she never has to run to the grocery store in the middle of cooking to pick up something she forgot. She plans all the meals for a whole week and goes to the grocery store just on Wednesdays.

"On Saturdays she bakes. They have a cookie jar in the kitchen, and she keeps it full of homemade cookies.

"She always has on her makeup, even at breakfast, and she goes to workout class three times a week and plays tennis to keep in shape. Her whole life is so well organized. You just can't imagine."

(No, I can't. More gloom.)

But with her next words, I cheered up.

"It was fun," she said, "but it's so nice to be home again where things are normal."

High School Daze

Teens are a great comfort in your old age, and they help you reach it faster, too.

—ancient Chinese proverb

By the time a child reaches high school, his mother has grown so old he can't do a thing with her. By the time he reaches high school, he also notices right away that his mother has conspired with his teachers to create rules and regulations and all manner of unreasonable demands that are designed to prevent his having a good time.

The wily teen-ager will manage to have a good time anyway.

The high school years are a time of education—yours, and of pranks and high jinks—theirs. And as you count your gray hairs, you find yourself praying for graduation day to arrive—which it does, all too soon.

Oh, for the Life of Everybody Else

There's a certain person I'm dying to meet. My children know this person well. In fact, they know the whole family.

This individual is male or female, depending on convenient circumstance, and is of an age ranging anywhere from 14 to 18.

The person's name is Everybody Else.

This fortunate soul leads an existence unfettered by rules, unhampered by curfews and unwatched by the careful eye of parent or guardian. From the teen-age standpoint, Everybody Else leads a life of sheer bliss.

Everybody Else gets to stay out late. Everybody Else has unlimited use of the family car and gets to strike out up the Interstate to Atlanta for rock concerts, returning home in the morning's dark and tiny hours.

Everybody Else has company whenever he or she wishes, whether or not there is school tomorrow, and Everybody Else does no chores. Everybody Else has tons of new outfits and lots of dates.

It must be delightful to be Everybody Else.

"Where are you going?" I asked about 10 p.m. on a recent Friday night as my two daughters headed out the door, giggling and jingling the car keys.

"We're going to the pizza place," they responded. "Everybody Else is going."

"When will you be home?"

"Midnight."

"That's too late," said I, ever the wet blanket. "You need to be in at 11:30."

"Aw, Mom, Everybody Else gets to stay out til midnight."

You see what a heavenly existence Everybody Else leads.

I would like to meet Everybody Else's parents. For one thing, I would like to meet anybody who would name a child Everybody. For another, they must be very easygoing folks since Everybody is allowed to do just as he or she pleases.

Mr. and Mrs. Else, from the teen point of view, are ideal parents. They respect Everybody's privacy to the point that they don't ask tacky old questions like, "Did you wash your face and hands?" and, "Who are you meeting at the bowling alley?" They don't say, "What are your plans after school today?" and they don't ask, "Have you done your homework?"

I'm told they understand that things like curfews and homework stunt Everybody's growth and good times, interfering with the pursuit of fun and games.

I can't understand why I've never seen Mrs. Else listed as the Mother of the Year. She's such a paragon, she's obviously a shoo-in for the title.

On the other hand, Everybody Else has an unlucky cousin. His name is Nobody Else, and he's a friend of my son. Nobody Else leads such a rough life. Nobody Else's mother asks, "Have you fed the cats?" and "Have you taken out the trash?" Nobody Else's mother keeps her son home from the Pac-Man parlor on nights before tests. Nobody Else's mother says motorcycles are dangerous. Nobody Else's mother is so mean!

I have checked the phone book carefully, and I cannot find either Else family listed. I think I know why. Both of those mothers are very busy ladies, too busy to talk on the telephone, so they may not even have one.

Nobody Else's mother stays busy imposing hardships on her son, making sure he goes to bed on time and seeing that he eats his broccoli. And I've been told that Nobody Else's mother works for a newspaper, so she obviously holds down a full-time job on top of all the rest of her activities.

But Everybody Else's mother is the one I'd really like to meet. I want to find out how she manages to provide unlimited funds for Everybody's allowance and what she uses for wheels while Everybody is out cruising in the family car.

However, I'm afraid she'll never have time to look me up. She stays busy, too. Everybody Else's mother makes all the beds, cooks constantly and cleans the house all by herself since Everybody Else is out having fun all the time.

I guess I'll never meet the Elses. It's funny how my children have gotten to know them so well.

All Laid Out

It's that time of year again. The back yard is full of teen-age girls engaged in the annual ritual of "laying out" in the sun.

Forget all the grammar you ever knew. For years I have tried without success to correct this gross insult to the English language. I could retire and live in riches if I had a nickel for every time I've said:

"The term, if you must use it, is 'lying out,' and it sounds horrible at that."

The reply is always the same:

"Aw, Mom, nobody says 'lying out.' What we're going to do is lay out in the sun and get a tan."

I have been known to reply, "Girls lie, hens lay," but somehow this doesn't sound quite right either. In fact, it sounds worse. So, as the years go by, my protests become more and more feeble. I have about given up the effort and now content myself with: "Don't lie out too long or you'll get burned."

This is greeted by more "Aw, Moms, ... "

When you lay out, you are seeking a beautiful, golden brown, french-fried look. But there's more to laying out than just basking in the sun.

First there are the essential ingredients to be collected—a sunny morning, all the girlfriends you can round up, about three beach towels per person, a pitcher of iced tea and dozens of paper cups, at least three radios turned to top volume (no two radios can be tuned to the same station) and gallons of suntan oil.

On laying out days, my back yard looks like Lake Tobesofkee minus the lake and the sand. And with such lavish use of suntan oil, it smells like a coconut festival.

Commercially produced suntan oils are considered OK if that's all you have on hand. But the various lotions and oils are better when they're mixed with additives, including baby oil and all your mother's cooking oil from the kitchen.

Experts in the art of laying out have been known to use about a gallon of oil an hour in the belief that a better tan is produced by deep frying rather merely sauteing in the sunshine.

Non-essential for laying out, but preferred, are a telephone extension handy to the back yard for those important communications with men, some sandwiches and potato chips and a swimming pool.

If there's no pool, the hose and sprinkler will do for an occasional cooling down. It's nice to have your mother around to serve the snacks, refill the tea pitcher and turn the sprinkler on and off.

About midday, a dutiful mother will caution her charges, "You're getting awfully pink. Why don't you come inside and listen to records or something?" They pretend not to hear.

Acceptable laying out behavior includes manicuring your finger and toenails, plucking your eyebrows, or having someone trim your bangs. I've noticed that for these activities my nail file, nail polish, tweezers and scissors often disappear into the back yard. I can usually find them there several days later. Neighbors have looked at me strangely as I emerged from beneath the shrubbery with a pair of tweezers in my hand.

_ No one engaged in laying out ever admits that she now approaches, or even will approach, looking good, no matter how tan she becomes, how straight her bangs or glamorous her nails. The conversation runs in this vein:

"Oh, Gawd, I look awful. Look at these lily white legs (arms, shoulders, hands, etc.)"

"There is no hope. I look like:

a.) an accident. Call a nurse."

b.) a sheet of typing paper."

c.) I spent the winter under a rock."

It's part of the fun for each layer-outer to profess to be in possession of Macon's oldest, crummiest bathing suit, fattest thighs and greasiest, grungiest hair.

I personally have laid out (no pun intended) an astronomical sum for a teen-ager's new bathing suit, only to hear her on the very next day react incredulously to a friend's compliment with, "This old thing?"

A day of laying out has its inevitable aftermath. The layer-outers rise late the following morning, their faces frozen in grimaces of pain. They resemble cooked lobsters.

They walk bowlegged with arms extended and shoulders hunched. They periodically cool their T-shirts in the freezer and flinch if you approach. They dab themselves gingerly with cotton balls soaked in vinegar. They cast about for a scapegoat. Mother is handy.

"Whyyy did you let us lay out for such a long time?" they moan. "Whyyy didn't you tell us we'd get burned?"

And then come those famous last words, "I'll never lay out again."

Accidents Will Happen

Handling a crisis is a breeze. When a crisis comes (ever noticed how it crops up when you least expect it?), you just have to stay cool and collect yourself. That's how simple it is. Clams are envious of my calm in a crisis.

Take last week, for instance.

It was 7:15 a.m. It was raining. Still in my nightgown, I had poured a cup of coffee and was looking at the drippy scene outside my kitchen window and loathing the thought of going out to work.

The telephone rang. It was Sam. Sam is our teen-age neighbor who rides to school with my daughters. They had been gone about 15 minutes.

"We had a wreck," said Sam. Sam doesn't fool around with preliminaries.

Calmly, I turned over the coffee pot. My cup slipped out of my hand and shattered in the sink, splashing coffee all over me and the cat. Clutching the telephone receiver with both hands, I stepped on the cat's tail as I sank into the nearest chair.

"How bad?" I asked, my voice shaking with composure as I removed the cat's 18 claws from my shoulder where he was clinging and yowling.

No one was hurt, said Sam, but it was a pretty bad wreck. Another car had spun into them. He gave me directions to the scene.

I dashed to my room, wondering what to wear. I decided on my jeans, since they were draped conveniently over the back of a chair where I had tossed them the night before. To complete my ensemble, I selected the old sweater wadded up underneath them. I put the sweater on wrong-side-out. (I always wear my sweaters wrong-side-out to wrecks.)

As I ran through the kitchen, my son (who rides the school bus) was munching cereal and surveying the coffee-strewn ruins. I grabbed him by the arm, pulling him after me into the carport. "They had a wreck," I mumbled as I threw him into the front seat.

"Who did?" he asked, adding practically, "If we're going somewhere, don't you need your car keys and your shoes?" In a crisis he's almost as calm as I am.

He brought my car keys, shoes and wallet while I fumbled with the seat belt. Ignoring the driveway, I backed carefully down the front lawn.

In all the rain, it was hard to see very clearly.

"Try the windshield wipers, Mom," suggested my son. Good idea.

We sped to the scene—observing all traffic regulations, of course.

The place wasn't hard to find. Flashing blue lights marked the spot. Then I saw my car. It and another automobile were sort of welded together in a curious T-shaped blend of crushed doors, fenders, hoods and grills. Broken glass and hubcaps were strewn about on the pavement.

"This must be the place," I observed intelligently as I pulled to the curb, and we stepped out into the rain.

Sam's dad had already arrived. So had a very nice policeman. They, my girls, the driver of the other car and Sam were all there, waiting for me to take charge. I noticed, as raindrops trickled down the back of my neck, that Sam's dad had worn a hat and raincoat. Good thinking. I was glad that he and everyone else seemed to be as calm as I was.

I sat in the police car and thought about my out-of-commission, mashed-up car and all the miraculously unhurt children. I began thinking about how bad it could have been. All this time, the nice police officer was carefully explaining what you do when there's been a wreck. He talked for several minutes about having the car towed and contacting the insurance company. "And that's about all there is to it," he concluded.

"Huh?" I asked. In my state of composure, I had not been listening.

Later in the day, as I dealt with the wrecker service, the garage, the insurance people, X-rays and our doctor, I noticed that, calm as I was, it helped to smoke—a bad habit I have been considering dropping. I smoked about 500 cigarettes that afternoon, my hand wavering only slightly each time as I singed my hair and nose with the lighter. I also drank gallons of coffee, having missed my first cup of the day.

But I am really happy that I stayed so unperturbed. It was a good example for the kids.

"You did just fine, Mom," said my son, "except when you drove through the azalea bed. And did you notice that you had your shoes on the wrong feet?"

As I said, you just have to stay cool, calm and collected.

An 8!

OK, all you parents out there, today I will discuss physics tests. One physics test in particular.

My daughter, my middle child, took the test last week in school. Out of a possible 100 points, she scored an 8. That's not a typo. It's not an 80 with the zero left off. It's an 8.

"I had four other tests that day, and I just didn't have time to study physics," explained the failure, shrugging her shoulders helplessly as she handed me the paper with the large, red 8 at the top. "I knew I was going to flunk, so I just tried to write interesting answers."

"What did your teacher say?" I asked her.

"He didn't say anything except for me to get you to sign it."

I sat down and read the test. After I fainted dead away and came to again, I signed it.

Now I'm going to let you read it. The test was captioned "Heat and Work."

Problem No. 1: Describe the Joule experiment for determining the mechanical equivalent of heat.

Her answer: "Mr. Joule reached in the fire and pulled out a hot coal with his bare hand and he got a blister. Then he reached in and pulled out another coal with his other hand and got a blister just as bad. Therefore, the heat was equivalent. (Mr. Joule was a caveman.)"

Problem 2: Distinguish between an adiabiotic process and an isothermal process. Where does the energy for each come from?

Her answer: "An isothermal process has constant temperature. An adiabiotic process doesn't. The energy comes from the four basic food groups. You are what you eat."

Problem 3: Diagram, label the important components, and describe each step in the 4-stroke cycle engine.

Her answer: (Her diagram was a sketch of a bicycle with a six-pack of Coors in the basket.) "1. Put R foot on R pedal. 2. Put L foot on L pedal. 3. Pedal rapidly. 4. Go to Lake Tobesofkee."

Problem No. 4: How can entropy be used as a quantitative measure of a system's ability to do work?

Her answer: "Very easily and very well, thank you."

Problem No. 5: Diagram, label and describe the ideal heat engine.

Her answer: (Her diagram was a sketch of a wood-burning fireplace with a sleeping dog in front of it and a picture of Grandma on the mantel.) "This ideal heat engine is called a fireplace. The fire gives off heat, which is very cozy on a cold winter's night. It's nice to take a nap on the hearth. The sleeping dog makes a nice pillow because he can keep your head warm. The wood is the fuel for this dandy invention."

Problem No. 6: Describe how to increase the efficiency of the engine in Problem 5.

Her answer: "Make it do more work in less time."

Problem No. 7: Describe and give an example of a process which converts: a) work to heat, b) heat to work.

Her answer: Work to heat: "Run from Central High School to Lake Tobesofkee. You build up a good sweat, and by the time you get there you're just a bundle of heat." Heat to work: "When you get to Tobesofkee, you are so hot and exhausted that everyone feels sorry for you, and they carry you to the water and throw you in."

Problem No. 8: Define or identify the following:

Rumford. Her answer: "The kind of salad dressing they serve at Main Street."

Heat Sink. Her answer: "A mini hot-tub."

External combustion engine. Her answer: "The opposite of an internal combustion engine."

What I can't figure out is how she managed to get eight points.

Experiment in Fine Dining

"Don't we have a tablecloth?" asked my high school senior. She was rummaging through the linen chest in the dining room. "I need a white tablecloth—the kind with shiny white designs in the corners like Grandmother uses for Christmas dinner."

I dug down to the bottom of the drawer and dredged up my only damask cloth.

"Nifty," she commented, plucking it out of my hands. "Just what I wanted."

I plucked it right back again.

"Not so fast, kiddo," said I. "Why do you want my best tablecloth?" (The last time I turned a child loose with a white tablecloth, he fashioned it into a Halloween costume—with eyeholes cut out of the middle.)

"Some of us at school are having a picnic tomorrow," she replied. "We're going to dine on the school lawn, and it's going to be ever so formal."

I declined to send my best tablecloth to be spread upon the ground, no matter how elegant the occasion.

Instead, I offered a white sheet.

"Tacky," she said with a negative shake of her head.

"I knew I should have waited until you were at work," she added, sadly watching the damask cloth disappear back into the chest. "But how about some silver candlesticks? Aren't there some little ones we could use if we take very good care of them?"

I searched through the cupboard and handed her four very small candlesticks. They were not in mint condition.

"Those aren't silver," she commented. "They're greenish black."

"Beggars cannot be choosers," I told her. "I'll give you some polish, and you can shine them up."

She trailed me into the kitchen where I initiated her into the rites of silver polishing. I left her standing over the sink.

About half an hour later, she found me again. "I think we'll just need two candlesticks," she said. "Polishing silver is the pits. Besides, I have to cook."

Each of the picnic participants was bringing part of the meal, she explained, a sort of covered-dish affair, but on an elegant plane.

"I'm bringing instant mashed potatoes," she said.

I marveled that she wasn't willing to prepare real potatoes for such a classy occasion.

"Mom," she said in her patient, explaining-obvious-facts-to-mother voice, "I am no dummy. I have mashed potatoes before, and mashing real potatoes is work. Instant potatoes will do nicely."

The rest of the gourmet menu included steak, beans and tea, to be supplied by the five other members of the party.

All the next day, I was curious about the progress of the picnic. I wasn't sure school officials would allow the unauthorized dinner on the grounds, formal or not.

I shouldn't have worried. She came home all smiles.

"It was terrific," she reported. "One of the teachers gave us a rose for our centerpiece, and the annual staff photographer came and took our picture. Then everybody just stood around and watched us eat and wished they were us."

She was so happy, I decided not to correct her grammar.

They ate from plastic plates—"not disposable ones or paper plates," she emphasized, "real plastic. Remember, this was very formal."

And the menu was a smashing success: steak, the potatoes and tea.

"Ray was supposed to bring beans," she related, "but he ate them on the way."

The instant potatoes were well received although the group was somewhat hampered by a shortage of forks. "We just shared the two we had," she said.

And who supplied all the steak?

"Oh, there was just one steak. We split it six ways."

For dessert, she added, they had a granola bar. "Who brought the granola bars?" I asked.

"Hil did," she replied. "There was just one granola bar. We passed it around."

(I hope no one in the group had anything contagious.)

"And Camille brought a tablecloth," she added, "so we had everything we needed. It was so much fun, we're going to do it again next weekend."

I'm so pleased. I think it's such good training for young people to be exposed to formal dining.

Graduation Jitters

It was a day of wild anticipation. The graduation girl threatened numerous shenanigans, and her mother was nervous.

The almost-graduate was up with the birds, bubbly as a bottle of champagne and twice as noisy. She pounced upon her sleeping mother. It was 6 a.m.

"Only four people can spend the night tonight," she announced. "You need to get some dip and munchies and Cokes."

"Ummph," mumbled the mother, recalling that in a recent moment of insanity she had, indeed, approved a graduation slumber party.

"And will you take me and Susan out to supper?" After-graduation supper is a family tradition, and Susan is a best friend. The mother nodded.

"Good," said the grad. "I shall order lobster and a complementing white wine."

"You will not order wine," grumbled her mother. The graduate grinned her most mischievous grin.

"It's going to be hot today," she continued. "I'm going to wear shorts and a T-shirt under my gown."

Her traditionalist mother (that translates into square) struggled to a sitting position.

"You should wear a dress to graduation; you'll be the only person there in shorts."

"I'll be the only person who's comfortable," said the irrepressible one. (Almost-graduates do not mind contradicting their mothers.) "It's too hot to wear a dress, and who's going to know what I've got on under my gown anyway?"

Her mother could think of no answer; instead she crawled out of bed and hastened toward the comfort of the coffeepot. It was going to be a long day.

The almost-graduate skipped ahead of her. Humming "Pomp and Circumstance," she prepared her breakfast—chocolate ice cream, a Coca-Cola and buttered toast.

Her mother averted her eyes from this nauseating combination, gathered her wits, got dressed and went to the office.

From time to time during the day, the graduation girl telephoned with new ideas for the ceremony: She and three friends would form a chorus line on stage; she would carry a yo-yo; there would be fireworks.

"I'm not a bit nervous," she added gratuitously.

Her mother was.

At mid-afternoon the mother arrived home to find the graduation candidate fretting.

"That stupid cap makes my head look flat. I'm not going to wear it," she said.

"You have to wear your mortarboard," said her mother. "It's traditional."

"I'll take it off just before I go up on the stage," threatened the renegade.

A diversion prevented further argument. The doorbell rang, and flowers were handed in. Pleased, she placed them among her gifts.

"Tomorrow I'm sending out reminders to all those lazy people who haven't sent presents yet," she said.

"Susan's going with us," she announced a few minutes later as they got into the car. Her mother was juggling cap, gown, makeup, hairbrush, hair spray and pins.

"Susan's going to help me with my hair and help me finalize what I'm going to do when I get on stage."

"What are you going to do?" asked her worried mother.

"Never mind, Mom. All you have to do is go inside the auditorium and save Susan a seat."

Less than an hour later, the mother and Susan sat in the auditorium. The music began.

The about-to-be graduate marched sedately down the aisle, double file with the capped and gowned members of her class. The mortarboard was neatly in place. She smiled graciously, a picture of dignity.

The mother relaxed, just a little.

Then Susan whispered, "She said she's going to flash us the Vogue look."

Inwardly, the mother groaned. Surely not.

There was no chorus line, no yo-yo, no fireworks. But just after the handshakes and the diploma, the graduate paused. She looked out over the audience at Susan, raised her chin and struck a haughty pose, so fleeting it was barely noticeable (the mother hoped). Susan giggled. "The Vogue look; I can't believe she did it!"

Then it was over, and the Class of 1984 filed out. The graduate, looking otherwise ever so academic, grinned and winked as she marched past. No one could tell that under her gown she wore shorts and a T-shirt.

Mom and the Bomb

Dear Son:

Just a note to say I am getting along beautifully driving your ancient, treasured Mustang while you are away this summer.

My attempt to foist the Mustang off on your sister didn't work. She took one look at the stick shift, noted that there is no air conditioner and said, "Mom, no way am I driving that bomb."

So, she drives my car, with the air conditioner, automatic transmission and tape player, and I am driving yours.

I do have several questions I hope you can answer. First, did you forget to tell me there is no window-roller-upper on the driver's door? No problem, though. During the big storm I ran out and covered the window with a plastic trash bag. The interior stayed dry even though I got pretty damp.

And after they towed the car in (you must have forgotten to mention that a bolt had fallen out of the clutch), our friendly service station man was able to pull the window up with a pair of pliers.

The window is up permanently, at least until I get a new window roller and something called a regulator to go with it.

This is all right except it gets a little warm in the car since there is no air conditioner and, as you will recall, the interior is solid black.

Still, driving with the window closed helps to muffle the hot-rod rumbling you like so much. I know it's hard for you to understand why adults don't appreciate the swell noise, but that's the peculiar way we are.

When I was in college, I dated a guy who had an old ski boat that sounded a lot like your car. Do you think it needs a new muffler, or is it really supposed to wake sleeping children three blocks away?

Speaking of noise, you must have noticed that the horn doesn't work. I'm having it repaired just for safety, though I haven't needed it. The motor is so loud that pedestrians tend to scatter for cover even before the car comes into view.

Last week I had our old tape player installed in that hole in the dashboard. It looks classy, but the thrill diminished to some extent when I discovered the car's speakers are missing. Did you remove the speakers, and if so, where are they?

It's OK, though, because I can sing to myself as I drive. Besides, there's no way I can drive a stick shift car and operate the tape player at the same time. Because it takes one hand to steer and the other to change gears, I wouldn't have a hand free to turn on the tape player anyway, so it's all just as well.

Frankly, I think that an automobile with three pedals on the floor ought to be operated by someone who has three feet. Dealing with the clutch, the brake and the accelerator while shifting gears all at the same time has been an exciting experience. Drivers behind me have been excited, too. (I will have the rear bumper repaired or replaced.)

It's somewhat embarrassing the way the car lurches and hops when a traffic light turns green and I let out the clutch in low gear. People on street corners giggle and point, and pushy types behind me always honk.

Actually, shifting into second and third gear is not so bad, since the car is already in motion by the time I get to that part. It's just discouraging to have to start out again from the very beginning every time I come to another red light.

So to avoid embarrassment, I have been arriving at the office about 7:30 every morning, well ahead of the traffic rush. And I don't go home until almost dark, when the streets are mostly deserted. It makes for long days, but my supervisor is pleased that I seem so industrious.

Where is reverse? I have not been able to find reverse at all. I know it's supposed to be at the top left of the H carved on the gear-shift knob, but it doesn't seem to be there. By some chance, did you remove reverse, too?

Not to worry. I have solved the problem, at least for the time being. I simply do not go anyplace where I might have to back up. This pretty much eliminates parallel parking, unless I can find a whole string of empty parking spaces and glide into them, but I am saving lots of money since I can't park anywhere to go in and shop.

I must say I'd be less nervous if the fuel gauge worked. Didn't it bother you, never knowing when you might run out of gas?

Please reply soon. Hope you are having a pleasant summer.

Love,
Mom

"Dear Mom, Send More Money!"

College is a fountain of knowledge where some students go to drink, some to sip, but most just go to gargle.
—ancient proverb

Train up a child in the way he should go, and before you know it, he's gone. College brought new and exciting experiences. I learned to pack, unpack and repack an automobile in the dark of early dawn. I learned that all roads lead to Athens, but from Macon it's a two-hour trip any route you take. And I learned new and unusual ways to stretch a dollar.

As far as I can tell, my children are learning a great deal about beer and football and bridge.

One thing we all have learned is that, even across the miles, we can share each other's daily lives by mail and telephone and, now and then, on weekends and holidays.

Managing Mom Is Simple

It's only the uninformed, unthinking mother who believes she manages her children.

How To Manage Your Mother is a best seller waiting to be written by a teen-ager. If my 18-year-old would just go ahead and write it, I could retire and let her support me.

She certainly has enough material. Take for instance, my recent efforts to buy her a suit for college.

"Now that you're going to college, you need a suit," I told her.

"Why?" she asked, mystified. "Why can't I just have some more jeans?"

The why was that when I was college-bound, my mother said it was time for me to have a suit. It was a three-piece outfit called a "weekender." I still have the three-quarter length coat.

So, I gave my child the same answer my mother gave me: "It's just time for you to have a suit."

"Far out," she responded, wide-eyed. "Do you think I'll ever wear it?"

"Well, if you don't wear it at college, you can always use it for job interviews later." I said.

She didn't object. (One of the mechanisms of effective mother management is subtlety; immediate, strenuous objections are counter-productive.) So, she smiled as we headed out to shop.

Right away we found a suit. She tried it on—a beige jacket with slightly A-lined matching skirt.

The blouse was soft with a big bow at the collar. She wriggled into the ensemble, straightened the skirt and buttoned the jacket, and we both stood gazing into the mirror.

She looked older, more sophisticated in the suit. I thought sadly of how soon she would be leaving home and far away, trying her wings—unprotected, alone.

"I look different—all grown up, don't I?" she asked, craftily reinforcing my maudlin thoughts.

Then she wrinkled her nose. "It's too ruffly anyway," she said.

There wasn't a ruffle in sight.

"Well, I mean, the bow looks all fluffy," she explained. "And the skirt makes me look fat, fat, fat. Yuck."

She is a size 5/6. There's no way she looked fat.

"Yes, I do, too, look fat," she was pointing at her tiny, trim waistline. "Just look how I pooch out."

The offensive suit went back to the rack, and we moved on to the next store.

She didn't like the navy suits; she didn't like the gray ones.

"If I've got to have a suit, I want beige," she said. "With a straight skirt; no pooches."

Three stores later, I desperately searched through endless rows of suits, looking for something beige. Something straight. No pooches.

She left me to my own devices, alone and harried among the suits, while she wandered happily through the casual wear, covetously fingering the bulky sweaters and nubby slacks.

"Look at this, Mom," she was holding up a spinach green jumpsuit. "Wow! That's neat!"

Doggedly, I continued my search.

Five stores later I turned up a miracle. Beige. Slim skirt. No ruffles.

Silently, frowning, she obediently wriggled out of her jeans and into the ensemble. (Psychologists call this tactic "passive resistance.")

"It itches," she announced, inserting her finger in the collar and stretching her neck this way and that. "And I'm starving; it's way past lunchtime. Let's go get something to eat."

We went and got something to eat. (Let no one say I ever starved a child to find a suit.)

"You look tired," she said as we ate lunch. (The power of suggestion is one of the most widely used principles of mother management). I *was* tired, now that she mentioned it.

So, abandoning the suit search we went home, where I kicked off my shoes and fell upon the bed, exhausted. I began to doze, rows of beige and navy suits floating before my eyes.

Very soon, she appeared in the doorway, a smile of ineffable sweetness upon her face, a frosty glass of iced tea in her hand.

"Here, Mommy. You look so tired, I made you some tea," announced the artful one. "Poor, tired Mom." She sat on the edge of the bed. There was a delicate pause.

Then, the whammy: "You know," she said, as if she just thought of it, "since I looked so terrible in those suits, why don't I just use the money to get that cute jumpsuit instead. I could go back and try it on right now, and since you're so tired, you stay here and rest. I can just take your credit card with me."

What a marvelous idea. I handed over the credit card.

She was out the door before I recognized that mother management had worked again.

Lots and Lots of Fun

Does anyone have any suggestions for wrapping a laundry basket for mailing? How about an ironing board?

Last week I received an urgent request from my college freshman. She had been at school four days.

When I heard her voice on the telephone, I thought, "She's homesick, or she's out of money."

Wrong on both counts.

She just wanted me to send a few things she forgot when she left home. I got a pen and began to make a list. She needs her beach towel (she didn't say why), her ironing board and her iron. Would I just put them in the mail.

While I pondered the cost of mailing an iron, I asked how she likes college.

"Fun, Mom. Lots of fun. UGA is the neatest place, and Athens is really cool," she informed me. "There are so many parties! Did you know they have lots of parties here?"

Yes, I have heard that somewhere.

She still has a little money, she said, "enough to get through a couple more days." (I had hoped her initial installment would last at least through next week.)

The reason her money hasn't held out quite as long as she expected, she explained, is that she has discovered the campus bookstore.

"It's really a super place, Mom. All the notebooks have bulldogs on the covers, and I got a cute bulldog rug to go by my bed and a fuzzy little stuffed bulldog to sit on my pillow. You pull a string and he growls."

(How adorable. And she needed another stuffed animal; she only took 47 with her when she moved out.)

She said she has also bought a few books. I envisioned her staggering out of the bookstore with a load of textbooks, but she quickly corrected me.

They were paperback books, purchased, I assume, for pleasure reading in those rare, fleeting moments between parties. One of the books is *Sweet*

Savage Dream, she said. Another, "a really good one," is *Pirate's Captive Woman,* and the one she hasn't begun reading yet is *Love's Radiant Splendor.* All, I am sure, are really fine examples of literary achievement.

But back to her original problem.

"Please send me my laundry basket—I left it in my closet—and my box of laundry detergent. It's under my bed, I think."

I added those to the list and asked about her dormitory.

She loves her room. "Soule Hall is one of the oldest dorms, so the rooms are really big. There's room to spread stuff around." That's good; she's awfully talented at spreading stuff around. She'll need all the space she can get.

Her roommate, she added in a startling announcement, "is a girl." (I was startled because, frankly, I hadn't considered the possibility of the alternative. Now that she's brought it up, I'm glad they're still conservative at UGA.)

Turning to other important matters, I asked when classes began. She sounded vague. "When does what begin? Oh, classes. Oh, yeah, well . . .I don't know really. I think Thursday or Friday. I'll try to find out today, right after I get back from the beer party."

"Beer party?" My heart stood still.

"Don't worry, Mom. I hate beer. Beer tastes yucky."

How does she know?

"Speaking of beer, I need the mug on my desk that holds all my pencils. Send the pencils, too, and also my green T-shirt—the one with the rhinoceros on the front. I need the shirt by Friday; I want to wear it to a party. It's either in my closet or my dresser, or maybe it's in the laundry. I can't remember.

"And send some food, Mom, lots of food. I'm starving."

The food is for her refrigerator, she said. She rented a refrigerator, so now she wants something to put in it. She wants a couple of six packs of soft drinks, crackers, a jar of peanut butter and some chocolate chip cookies. "And a knife for the peanut butter," she added.

She instructed me to put everthing, including the iron, in the laundry basket, wrap it up and mail it as soon as possible.

"You'll probably have to wrap the ironing board separately," she informed me helpfully.

I may just put it all in the car and drive it to Athens. It probably would be cheaper. Easier, too.

A Weekend at Home

I have discovered the most expensive part of a college student's education.

It isn't the tuition, and it isn't the books. Those are minor. It isn't the cost of the wardrobe, although that runs a close second. And it certainly isn't the cost of those two frills, room and board. Never those.

The most expensive part of your child's education is The Weekend at Home. I discovered this last Friday, Saturday and Sunday.

"Hi, Mom, I'm home," she called out as she came through the back door.

Delighted to see her after her absence of four weeks, I made what my children refer to as "excited mother noises"—"You're so thin! Aren't they feeding you? What a cute new hairdo. Oh, I'm so glad to see you," etc.

I also wrapped her in a bear hug. She endured all this patiently, humming a little tune under her breath and wearing a "This, too, shall pass" expression while I hugged, kissed and exulted.

"I need five dollars to pay Edward for gas for the ride home," she announced after I had recovered my composure. "And I need six dollars for a ticket to the Producer's concert tonight."

I forked over eleven dollars.

She looked dismayed. "Can I have a little spending money? I'm sort of broke." I added five more dollars, and she whisked it all into her pocket.

"And I'd like to have the car this afternoon," she added. "Can you put some extra gas in it? I want to go see Lisa and Brian and check out the mall."

Out of cash at this point, I proffered my gasoline credit card, which disappeared like magic into the same pocket.

After demolishing several sandwiches and a pint of ice cream, she left.

"See you later; don't wait up," she sang out, slamming the door.

That was the last time I saw her on Friday.

At an uncivilized hour on Saturday morning, she woke me up.

"Let's go to the mall, Mom," she said. "We need to get me a jacket, and maybe I can find something to wear. I need some clothes."

Through my early morning fog, I noticed that she was wearing a new outfit. "Oh, it's Aimee's," she said. Aimee is her roommate. "I'm wearing her clothes this weekend. She has tons of clothes. I don't have any."

I mentioned the mounds of shirts, blouses, skirts, jeans, slacks and dresses she took to school.

"But those are old," she argued. "We bought those last summer."

(We bought them six weeks ago.)

I informed her it will be necessary for her to wear her "old" clothes for a while yet.

"I knew you were going to say that," she replied. "I just thought I'd try."

But she did need a jacket. So, I got up and dressed to go shopping. After a morning-long search, she found the right jacket—a red and black jacket.

"Neat colors," she remarked, watching me write the check. "Let's go get a pizza. I'm starving."

To the local pizza parlor we went, where I wrote another check.

Then she volunteered to let me take her grocery shopping for snacks.

A band of gypsies could live for a month on what she purchased (rather, what she selected; I purchased it): powdered lemonade mix, a jar of peanut butter and one of jelly, bread, cookies, soft drinks, coffee, tea bags, artificial sweetener and a jumbo box of animal crackers.

Back home again, she emptied the cabinets of canned goods, leaving only the beets, candied yams and French-cut beans—a total of six cans.

"That should hold us for a while," she said, surveying her three bulging grocery sacks. I wondered out loud what the three of us left at home would eat.

"That's no problem, Mom," she said. "You can always go back to the grocery store. Remember, you have a car, and I don't."

The next day we packed the car with her groceries, the new jacket and some "old" clothes she had overlooked when packing up for her first trip to school. We filled up the gas tank again and headed for Athens.

On the way, I found out that moms don't drive to Athens free of charge. My weekend spending spree wasn't over yet. Not quite.

"I'd really like one more square meal before I have to endure the culture shock of cafeteria food," announced my thin and starving passenger. "So, when we get there, why don't you take me and Aimee out for a big supper?"

The Long Distance Operator

Show me a mother whose child has just called home from college, and I'll show you a woman whose nerves are so frayed she couldn't get a UL listing if she tried.

The call comes collect, of course.

"Hi, Mom, this is me," says our Athens correspondent. "Just wanted to let you know we got our phone bills here in the dorm this afternoon.

"This girl down the hall from me had a bill of—just wait till I tell you how much—it was $280. $280! Can you imagine that? She's been calling her boyfriend a lot. He goes to Washington State. Boy, is her dad steamed!"

"And how much," I inquire delicately, "was your own telephone bill?"

"Lots better than $280, Mom. It really wasn't too bad, but I do realize I've called you collect a lot of the time."

Yes, that's true. And I'm considering taking a second mortgage on the house.

"Well, how much was it?" I ask with a minor flicker of arrhythmia. A seasoned mother, I recognize the old phone-bill-down-the-hall ruse.

She ignores the question.

"Speaking of telephone bills, Mom, I have a joke for you. It's a real turkey. You'll love it. Who is Alexander Graham Bell Pulaski? Give up?"

I give up.

"He was the first telephone Pole. Get it? Telephone Pole? Do you understand it, Mom? Isn't it awful? It's so horrible, it's cute."

The cat's pajamas, but I'm waiting to hear about the phone bill, Witty One.

She bubbles right along. I am increasingly nervous.

"Mom, college is fabulous. I want you to know I am taking it seriously and that I really appreciate for the first time in my life what a sacrifice you're making and how important my education is to my development as a contributing human being. Really."

(Have you ever noticed that gray hairs make noise as they sprout?) She rattles on.

"And I never fully appreciated football before. It's a terrific game—except the Auburn game wasn't so hot. We cried. It was just excruciating.

"But you'll be proud of my grades—sort of. I'm not flunking out or anything, and anyway I wasn't expecting that political science test.

"Pop tests are the pits; just one can ruin your whole average in one stupid hour. Besides, we have political science at 7:50 a.m. That grosses me out. I can hardly prop my eyes open."

I am frantically twisting the phone cord into little pretzels. "What are your grades?" I ask, my voice shaky.

"Oh, they're OK, Mom. Don't worry. By the way, I meant to ask you, how do you get ball point pen out of a coat?"

"Which coat?"

"My new one—the one for church and parties. There's just a little bit of ball point pen, but it's right down the back. I was scratching my shoulder, and I forgot the top was off the pen."

My heart sinks fast as the barometer reading in a tropical storm. Her brand-new, lovely cream colored coat . . .

"Take it to the cleaners quick and what are your grades?" I persist. "And what was your phone bill?"

"Oh, by the way, Mom, speaking of going to the cleaners, I opened a checking account this week. I've written lots of check—writing checks is fun. My new checks have pictures of kittens on them.

"But could you send me $500 pretty quick? If I keep $500 in my account, I don't have to pay the bank $5 every month."

Why, of course, my precious treasure. Why didn't you ask sooner? I'll just run out back to the money tree and pick a few $100s. I think I noticed a few of them greening up nicely a couple of days ago.

"And there's something in my new checkbook I don't understand. It's the other little booklet, the one with lines on it. On the front it says 'Check Record.' Am I supposed to do anything with that?"

As the blood drains from my face. I lie down right where I am on the floor, clutching the telephone receiver to my ear. I need oxygen.

"Tell me what your phone bill was, what your grades are and how many checks you've written. Tell me now, right now, before you tell me any more jokes or say anything else."

"Oh, it's really not that bad, Mom. I just wanted you to be prepared. The phone bill was $10.50, and I have a C in political science. My other grades are an A and a B, so don't worry.

"They explained to me at the bank how the check record works. And I really don't expect the $500, but I wondered if I could have maybe $25 for a few extras next month?"

When she graduates, she should go to work for the telephone company. Ma Bell won't even have to train her. It's obvious she's become a long distance operator.

Celery, Carrots and Unsweetened Tea

The birthday girl stormed into the kitchen, slammed the back door and threw her wallet on the kitchen table.

She had been shopping for a bathing suit. Somehow I knew what was coming.

She stamped her foot and glared at me.

"I am fat, fat, fat," she declared, tears in her eyes. "I look so gross it's just gross. When I graduate, I can get a job as the fat lady in the circus."

A bathing suit was what she wanted me to give her for her 19th birthday; so, I had sent her on a last-minute shopping trip before she returned to college after spring break.

For weeks she had been poring over magazines, oohing over this year's crop of bathing suits.

As far as I have been able to determine from looking over her shoulder, swimwear this year involves a couple of strings that tie together a few tiny triangles of strategically located fabric.

Considering the amount of material involved, bathing suits should cost about $2.98. They don't, of course.

Her "last year's" bathing suit, which was admired and coveted for several months before she saved up enough to buy it, is now said to be "ugly, blah, lumpy, faded, funny looking, shrunk-up, uncomfortable, old-fashioned and gross."

And she had been looking forward to her birthday so that she could make her appearance in one of the new models.

Of all the people in our family, she is the one who is definitely not fat, fat, fat. She is instead, slim, slim, slim. I started to tell her that but was interrupted as she read my thoughts.

"Don't say it, Mom. Just don't say it. I can see it in your face. You're going to try to tell me I'm not fat. I don't want to hear it. It's not true. I have rolls and rolls of ugly globs everywhere. I am a beach ball, an elephant. In a bathing suit I look like King Kong. If I fell out of bed, I'd bounce."

She stormed out of the kitchen, and I heard her bedroom door slam.

Her brother ambled in, in search of a snack.

"What's wrong with Attila the Honey?" he asked, peering into the refrigerator and emerging with the roast for supper, two apples and a gallon of milk.

"Put the roast back," I told him. "She's been trying on bathing suits."

He nodded knowingly, returning the roast to the refrigerator shelf. He rummaged around and found a whole pie instead.

"Oh," he said. "And now she thinks she's fat and ugly, and she's going on a diet of celery and carrots and iced tea and do Jane Fonda exercises six times a day."

I asked how he knew that.

"I remember when she tried on bathing suits last year. It was the same thing." He sat at the kitchen table, demolishing the pie, the apples and the milk.

His sister stomped back into the kitchen again, looking trim in leotards and leg warmers.

"Just look at him, stuffing down food," she exploded, pointing at her brother. He tried to look innocent as we observed the crumbs of pie, the dregs of milk, the two apple cores. "He eats all the time, and he never gains an ounce. It's revolting."

With a pained and noble expression, she continued.

"I am going on a diet of celery and carrots and iced tea," she declared. "Celery for breakfast, carrots for lunch and iced tea for supper. And I'm going to do the Jane Fonda workout six times a day."

In the meantime, I inquired, what was she going to do about a bathing suit for the summer?

"Nothing," was the response. "I'm wearing turtle necks and baggy jeans all summer. I'm staying indoors where no one can see me. I'm staying in my room. You'll have to push celery and carrot sticks under the door. I'm not coming out until I'm shaped like Christie Brinkley."

"But what about your tan?" I asked. Every spring and summer she works on a tan.

She looked distraught at the thought. "I guess I won't get one this year. What's the point of being tan if you're ugly and fat? Who wants to go out with a tan hippopotamus?"

She retired dramatically to her room and slammed the door. Silence ensued while my son rummaged through the bread box. "Don't worry, Mom," he advised me as he returned to the kitchen table, a box of cookies in his hand. "Last year she said the same thing. But she only stayed in her room till she got hungry."

What? My Child?
A Dummy?

Out of the dark sounds the shrill ringing of the telephone.

I fumble with the bedcovers, then wreak havoc across the bedside table, knocking papers and books to the floor as I grope for the receiver.

"Hi, Mom," chimes the cheery voice of my firstborn. "Did I wake you up? I'm sorry; I didn't realize it was so late."

"What time is it?" I inquire groggily, falling back upon my pillow and struggling to stay awake. It seems I have been asleep for hours.

"Well, actually, now that I look, it's 2 a.m.," she says. "I'm really sorry I woke you up; we were playing bridge, and I just didn't realize how late it is. I just called to say hi."

Well, of course, I am delighted to receive a call at any hour from the campus of the red and the black, and so I try my best to be alert and conversational.

"Who was playing bridge?" I ask.

"Oh, me and three girls across the hall."

From long-established habit, I make the grammatical corrections I've been making for years: "Three girls from across the hall and I, right?"

"No, Mom, you're not here. It's me and some girls in the dorm."

She'll never be an English scholar, but I decide to drop the subject. I think you should not correct the grammar of a child who bothers to call home just to say hi.

While she may graduate from college with her pronouns misplaced, at least she's thoughtful. And she is learning something, if only to play bridge.

"So, how are things going?" I ask.

"Everything's even better than last year," she enthuses. "I think that's because I'm more adult now. Everything's wonderful, except I lost my checkbook. I think I lost it in smelling during breakfast, and—"

I interrupt: "In smelling?"

"Yeah," she says, "smelling. Smelling Hall. It's the cafeteria where we eat. It's actually Snelling, but we call it Smelling."

How adult.

"Anyway I can't find the checkbook anywhere, and the worst part is that my student ID card was in it. So, I had to go to the bank and close my account, and now I've got to have another ID made and open another checking account, and it's a big hassle. I had to go to the bank yesterday instead of play bridge.

"And I know that as soon as I get it all worked out, my checkbook will show back up. It's probably under my bed. That's the way life goes."

Well, she's not learning much grammar, but she apparently is learning something about life. Along with the bridge.

She bubbles on:

"But you know what's happened that's really neat? All of a sudden I understand football. In the Clemson game, I realized I knew what was going on the whole time. Wow, what a game!

"Mom, you really should have been here. Athens was a zoo that night. Everybody was just going bananas, and I've never seen so many happy, drunk people all over the place. It was wild.

"I never realized before how important it is to win a football game."

She is going to graduate with incorrect pronouns and a checkbook in smelling, but never mind. She's learning about life, bridge and football.

"How are classes?" I decide the conversation should turn serious.

"Classes?" she hesitates. "Oh, classes. Yeah, well, they're OK; I just don't let them interfere, you know? All my classes are early in the morning; so, I get them out of the way before lunch. Then, except for band practice, the rest of the time we just do things—you know, go out and eat, play bridge, go shopping, whatever."

"When," I ask in my most tactful voice, "when do you study?"

"I knew you were going to ask that," she says. "Mom, don't worry. There's lots of time for studying. You can study while you're the bridge dummy or while your nail polish is drying, and you can study while you're doing your laundry. Just yesterday, I read *Paradise Lost* during the rinse cycle.

"But I've gotta go, Mom. I just had a few minutes; so I wanted to call and say hi."

"Taking a break from studying, huh?" I ask.

"Studying?" she hesitates again. "Oh, no, Mom, I'm not studying. I had a few minutes because I was the bridge dummy.

"Now, I've really gotta go 'cause it's my deal."

Some Really Good Reasons

First, I let her take the car to school because, "It's really necessary, Mom, for my education class, and it's just for two weeks anyway."

Six weeks later, the following letter arrived, and I realized I'm not raising a schoolteacher; I'm raising a lobbyist.

"Dear Mom,

"Can we discuss the car? It has been neat having the car at school these past few weeks. Thanks for letting me bring it up here. I don't know how I would have gotten my observations done for education class without it, but with it I was able to zoom right around to all the schools.

"It seems strange to me that you can get credit for observing little kids in their classrooms. All they're doing is the same dumb stuff we did in third grade.

"Anyway, now that my observations are over, I guess you will be wanting the car back home.

"Mom, there are some really good reasons for letting me keep the car at least until the quarter ends.

"For one thing, I can go to the grocery store, and snacks are lots cheaper there than in our machines here in the dorm. It saves lots of money.

"For another thing, it is much safer for me to drive than walk around town, particularly at night. I know you are always concerned for my safety, and just remember, I can lock myself inside the car. Now that I have grown accustomed to the car, I feel truly unprotected on foot. So, please consider my safety when you are making up your mind.

"Another safety factor is that with the car I don't have to bum rides from people I don't know well. I have never thought it was safe to ride around with people that I hardly know from other parts of the dorm. After all, one of them could turn out to be a mugger.

"And having the car is very good for my social development since I can pay back the people who drove me around last year. When everybody wants to go out for supper, now I can drive. And everyone likes to ride in my car since it's red, which is a very popular color on this campus.

"And when I need to come home weekends, I can just drive myself. I know it has been easier on you not having to be on the road between Macon and Athens, and I feel better knowing you're not out driving around by yourself.

"And having the car here at school is helping me become a more responsible person, which you always said is one of the goals of going to college anyway. I budget my money for gas and keep the oil checked and am not letting the car stay filled up with trash for long periods of time.

"I'm sure that when you think about it, you will agree that having a car here on campus is good training for me for that time in the not-so-distant future (I hope) when I will have my own car to take care of.

"Having the car has also been a chance for me and Sabra to practice sharing since, as soon as I got the car here, she began thinking up reasons to use it. Sabra and I have become lots closer from having to work out who gets the car. It is really good for us, and we have sisterly conversations, which is important since we live in different dorms (apart for the first time in our lives). It's true we have had a few fights, but just little ones and only when she was being a jerk.

"Speaking of Sabra, did you know she changed her major from journalism to education? As soon as she found out you were letting me use the car for education observations, she switched. And winter quarter she is going to take the same education course I am taking now, so don't be surprised if she tells you she needs the car winter quarter.

"In the meantime, this quarter is so nearly over (only another month or so) that there isn't much point in bringing the car home. You would hardly have time to notice it's there.

"Please, please, please, can we keep the car?

"Love,
"Nancy"

"Don't Worry,
I'll Just Starve"

"Dear Mom,

"Usually I just call, but I decided to write you a letter instead of calling this week since my bank account is kind of low, and my telephone bill this month was kind of high.

"Actually, the telephone bill was very surprisingly, astoundingly high, and it came at a bad time since I had just bought a new shirt and a tape for my cassette player. I wasn't thinking about the telephone bill when I was buying the new stuff, and it was really unexpected because I had just paid the phone bill from last month.

"So now I have sort of a problem.

"I don't mean that you need to send me extra money or anything like that. (I'm not the kind of college student who just writes home when she needs money.)

"I can make it and pay the phone bill, too, if I eat every single meal in the dining hall for the next two weeks and don't buy any snacks.

"And I won't buy any coffee out of the coffee machine while I'm studying late at night even though it's terribly hard to stay awake and study without coffee. I keep dozing off, which is not an efficient way to study. And when everyone else is having a good time drinking coffee together, it smells good and makes me want some, too. But I will just struggle through without it, all by myself.

"Of course, the dining hall food is yucky, but not eating will help me lose weight. It will be good for my diet and my willpower. I already feel thinner and have only felt dizzy a few times, mostly late in the afternoon when I have been running around all day with little nutrition to sustain me.

"And it's embarrassing when my stomach growls in class.

"But don't worry about me. I will be just fine. One thing that is good is that we had a hall party in the dorm last night, and I was on the cleanup committee. So, I got to keep some of the leftover potato chips and a few

traces of dip. I am saving them on my window sill in case I have an un-
bearable snack attack during my days of starvation. Even if they're stale, it
will be better than nothing.

"We've been having mid-terms, which is OK I guess since I'm too broke
to do anything but study anyway. I did OK in English, but German was a
crunch. I don't know what my grade is yet, but I'm nervous. I don't understand how a whole nation of people can speak German to each other
and understand what anyone is saying. Even little kids in Germany speak
German, and here I am in college, having trouble saying Volkswagen.

"Did you know that the German way to say Volkswagen is Folksvagen?
It means "people car." Just because they invented it, the Germans say it that
way, so we have to say it that way in class. I keep forgetting and saying it
the good old American way. Why can't the Germans just say Volkswagen
like everybody else?

"I'm not washing any clothes for a while either. That way I can save
more money toward my phone bill. No one really can tell whether you've
washed your jeans anyway. They don't show dirt. Shirts and underwear are
more of a problem. But I think I can get by for two weeks, especially if I
use some of my spring stuff toward the end. And I'll be OK in short sleeves
as long as the weather doesn't get too cold. If it gets too cold, I'll have to
cut classes unless I find my jacket that's been lost for two weeks.

"My friend Jennifer down the hall has a coffee pot in her room and some
cereal. She said she will share with me until things get better. Jennifer is a
very nice and generous person, and she knows what I'm going through because she had a similar problem once.

"She told me that once last year she had a great big telephone bill, even
bigger than mine. She starved for two days, but then her mother sent her
a great big surprise check, and she was able to pay the bill and even have
something to eat, too.

"Jennifer believes I should write and ask you for extra money, but I don't
think I should. I think I should be able to get along on the little bit that
you send me regularly, even if it is sometimes very hard.

"Don't worry about me. I will be fine. I have to close for now because
I've got to find someone to borrow a stamp from so I can get this letter in
the mail.

"What is going on at home? I hope that y'all are warm and have plenty
to eat.

"Love,
"Nancy"

"How'd You Ever Guess?"

"Dear Mom,

"Hey, wow! Thanks for the check. It was a real surprise.

"You must have been reading between the lines of my last letter to figure out that I really needed some money. It's just amazing the way moms can always tell things like that.

"I went right to the post office and sent off my telephone payment so they won't disconnect my phone. It would be terrible not to have a phone because then I could never call home and say hey to you and the cats.

"Then I went to the grocery store and bought some food for me and a box of cereal for Jennifer. You remember I told you about my friend Jennifer down the hall. She's the one who shared her cereal with me last week while I was starving because of no money. So, I paid her back with one of those big packages of little boxes of cereal that you can eat right out of and not have to wash a bowl.

"I got some cookies, a couple of candy bars and lots of potato chips and dip for me. And I also bought some carrots and bananas and apples because I think it's important to consider nutrition when you're a growing teen-ager.

"Which brings me to a point I have been wanting to bring up. Don't forget that my birthday is coming up pretty soon. It's just 109 days away, and by the time you get this letter it will be just about 107 days away, and I thought I'd mention it sort of early because of what I want.

"I was thinking that since you let Harley buy a car just recently, maybe you would let me get one. Someone sent me the column you wrote about how mature and responsible we are, and I think that you are certainly right about that.

"It would be really convenient to have a car at school. That way, I could just whiz home whenever I wanted to without looking around for a ride. It would be nice to be able to go over to Atlanta to shop and maybe hit a few concerts at the Omni now and then. To say nothing of not having to walk to the grocery store and lug those heavy sacks back to the dorm.

"I envision something like a Mustang or a small, inexpensive Mercedes. It could even be a used one as long as it still looks good.

"I realize a car would be sort of a problem since I don't have a job, but you could pay for the car, and I could pay you back after I graduate and begin working. It's kind of embarrassing to have your little brother who is only in high school be a car owner and not be a car owner yourself, especially when you know you are such a mature person and could handle it so well.

"I have the feeling you are probably going to say no, but I wish you would think about it very carefully first and remember that I am making good grades (except in German).

"Frankly, I wish I had never heard of German. One of the problems is that German class is at 7:50 in the morning, and I am not at my very best that early. I can hardly say hello at 7:50, and in German hello is 'Guten Morgen.' It has little tongue trills, which are very difficult to manage before breakfast. I knew I should have taken Portuguese instead. Portuguese has lots of irregular verbs, but it meets at 10 o'clock, which is a much more reasonable hour.

"By the way, can you send me some things? Now that it's getting to be spring and the sun is out, everyone is laying out to get a tan. You wouldn't believe what it looks like up here these days. There are bodies lying all over the tennis courts, just like at the beach.

"So, I need my bathing suit (unless you would like for me to get a new one) and some sun screen for my nose (I think there's still some from last summer in the bathroom cabinet). Also if you could send the rest of my tapes, they're under my bed. And my beach towel, the one with Donald Duck on it.

"Anyway, thanks for the money. Things look much better now that I have some food. It's amazing how much better you feel when you have money on hand.

"If you had some extra money around, you could send it, and I could open a savings account with it, just in case I ever have a telephone bill problem again.

"Love,
"Nancy

"P.S. The cookies you sent were very good. Also it was a surprise that you baked them since you have never seemed to be a very domestic mom. You could send some more if you want to."

Moving Home For Summer

Our house looks as if we have opened an indoor flea market.

Cardboard boxes, suitcases, clothes, books and kitchen appliances are strewn in a path from the front porch to what we usually refer to as "the middle bedroom."

Spillover—luggage, three clarinets, two rolls of posters and piles of sheets and towels—covers most horizontal surfaces in the bathroom and what we usually refer to as "the back bedroom."

We are eating in the kitchen because the dining room table is piled high with records, tapes, David Bowie posters, one snare drum, two coffeepots, a hotplate and two years of back issues of *Vogue*.

I have two bedtime companions sleeping in my room at night because their own beds are lost under great pyramids of unfolded laundry.

There is still one radio, a set of hot curlers and a stack of term papers in the back seat of my car.

The cats have retreated to the crawl space under the house because their usual napping spots—sofas, chairs and beds—are inaccessible.

The girls are home from college.

They're going to clean the whole mess up "real soon, Mom," but so far other things—mainly the doorbell and telephone—have conveniently intervened.

Here are some of the things I learned on that memorable day last week when I moved them home:

● It takes six hours, one haul-it-yourself trailer, one midsize automobile, both girls and one mom to move two girls out of two dormitories and home again.

● If you want to be perfectly miserable, try staggering repeatedly down dormitory stairs under heavy boxes and armloads of winter woolens in temperatures near 102 degrees.

● Backing a haul-it-yourself trailer out of a dormitory parking lot crowded with cars, parents, students and their belongings is not next to impossible. It is impossible. And it adds color to your vocabulary.

● Dainty young ladies who spend two hours loading a haul-it-yourself trailer develop the appetites of Pittsburgh Steelers and ask incessantly, "How soon can we eat?"

● A mother who participates in an afternoon of such activity will sleep exceedingly well for about 12 hours afterwards.

As usual the two college women, as they prefer to be called, each went about the task of packing in her own distinctive way.

"I threw a lot of stuff out," explained the younger of the two as I marveled that she had only three suitcases, two large cardboard boxes, hanging clothes, two pillows and an electric fan.

What's more, she had managed to change the time of a final exam so that she and her sister could come home on the same day.

Not only that, she had engaged her roommate, the roommate's gentleman friend and her own gentleman friend to help us carry her belongings down to the car. We were loaded in a matter of minutes.

"This is going to be lots easier that I thought," I remarked, forgetting to knock on wood as we headed for her sister's dormitory.

I spoke entirely too soon. From the door of her room to the door at the top of stairs, a distance of some 15 feet, was a jumble of my firstborn's belongings. The rest was still in her room, still unpacked.

"I ran out of boxes," she explained when we finally located her, playing cards down the hall in a friend's room. "But," she added brightly, "I'm almost ready."

My heart, as they say, sank. Her perception of "almost" has always ranged somewhere from two hours to two weeks from now.

An hour and a half and many miles of steps later, we had loaded the trailer and car, but a couple of boxes remained on the sidewalk.

"We're not going to have room for it all," I predicted glumly.

My eldest frowned as she peered into the jam-packed trailer. "There is still plenty (she pronounced it "pull-en-ty") of room in there, Mom," she declared.

So, we shifted things around until we made room for the remaining two boxes.

Too tired to speak, we wedged ourselves into the car. Then: "Wait," cried the pack-rat, opening her door again as I pulled away from the dorm. "My stuffed animals! I forgot them! They're in the closet." And she ran back inside, emerging in moments with two plastic garbage bags filled with fuzzy friends.

She had to hold them on her lap all the way home.

"Stuffed animals," she remarked two hours later as we pulled up in front of the house, "are very warm."

Family Album

If a picture is worth a thousand words, why am I doing all this writing? What follows is about 18,000 words worth of family snapshots. You can be looking at them while I go whip up a snack.

*Yes, they're all mine. No, they're not triplets. A lapful of Nancy (left),
Harley and Sabra*

*A bucket and hose were always favorite summer-day playthings, and they loved to
wash the puppy*

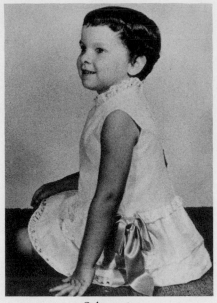

Sabra, 3 1/2

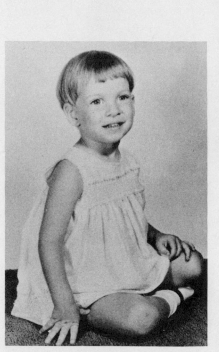

Nancy, 2

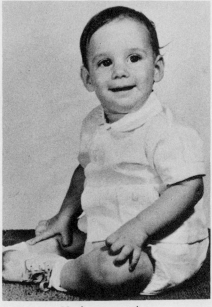

Harley, 8 months

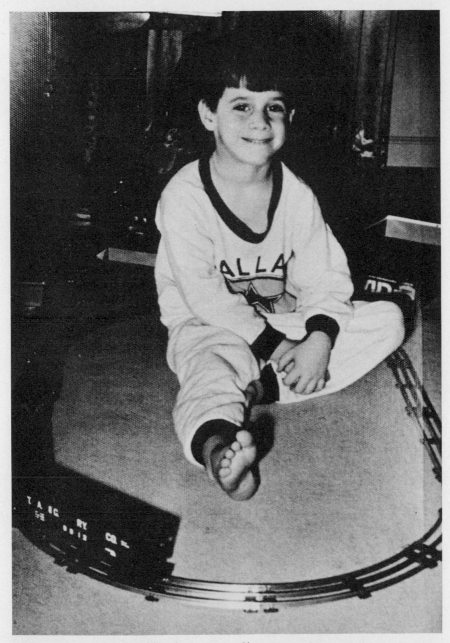

Harley and his electric train, Christmas morning 1974

Grandmother Sydney   Granddaddy Lloyd

Sabra's big catch. She wanted to keep them for pets

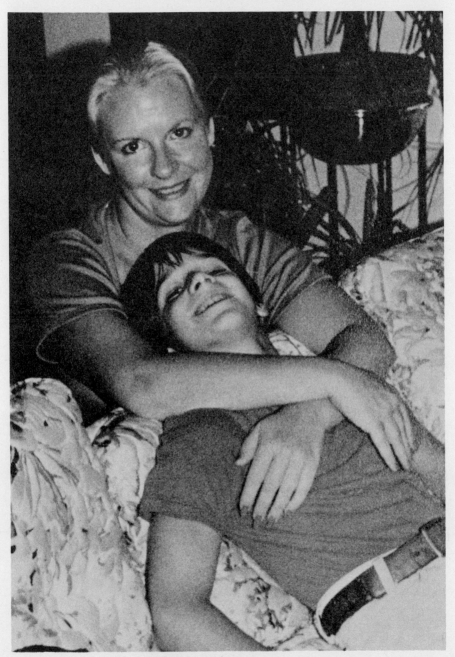

Harley with Mom, 1978

Sabra and High Society Man, who never would put his ears up for the camera

Max (in front) and Stumpy in their usual "We're waiting patiently for supper" pose

But I cleaned it up last month!"
A view of Sabra's room
in Soule Hall

Nancy the graduate wearing robe and shorts.
This was just moments after the
"Vogue" look

Uga watching Sabra,
the late-night snacker

Sabra, 17

Nancy, 17

Harley, 17

Christmas

Christmas at our house has always been a time for secrets and whispering, excitement and giggles, snooping and rummaging and mysterious packages hidden away. Some of our Christmas memories are funny ones; all of them are happy. And through the years, I have learned that Christmas spent with one's grown-up children is just as joyful as those long-ago Christmases when they were small.

'Twas the Night Before . . .

Getting into the spirit of Christmas one night long ago, I asked the children if they would like to hear "A Visit From St. Nicholas."

The children like to be read anything, so we gathered in front of the fire after supper with the big book of poems, and I began.

'Twas the night before Christmas
And all through the house
Not a creature was stirring,
Not even a mouse."

"What's a twas?" someone asked.

I explained.

"What were they stirring?" someone else asked.

"They weren't stirring," I explained. "They were all being very still and quiet."

"On Christmas Eve? Yech," remarked the wiggliest member of my brood, fidgeting.

"The stockings were hung by the chimney with care,
In hopes that St. Nicholas soon would be there."

Everyone smiled. They KNOW about that part.

"The children were nestled all snug in their beds,
While visions of sugarplums danced in their heads."

"What does visions mean?" asked one.

"It means they had their eyes checked," replied her sister, the one who recently got spectacles.

"While I in my kerchief and Ma in her cap
Had just settled down for a long winter's nap."

"Nap?" they asked in horrified tones. With my crowd, naps rate right up there with Castoria and hair washes.

"Is a kerchief like pajamas?" one wanted to know.

I nodded vaguely. Actually, I've never been too certain about that part myself.

I went on.

"*. . . tore open the shutters and threw up the sash . . .* "

"He threw up!" they all cried in unison. Obviously they thought this was a very strange story.

"Did his mama call the doctor?" was the next question.

I explained about window sashes, and continued. We did all right until I got to the part about,

"As dry leaves that before the wild hurricane fly
When they meet with an obstacle, mount to the sky,
So up to the house-top the coursers they flew,
With a sleigh full of toys and St. Nicholas, too."

Encouraged by their interest, I continued, only to be interrupted by more questions.

"What's a courser, Mama?"

"What's a bound? I thought he came down the chimney with a sack."

"What does 'down on a thistle' mean?"

I explained all, and read on, winding up with, *"Happy Christmas to all and to all a Good Night"* just as the telephone rang.

The youngest answered.

"Hi, Grandmother. Mama just read us this neat poem," he announced with enthusiasm. "It's all about Santa Claus and this boy who threw up, and then they had a hurricane that blew the sleigh up on top of the house. Then the boy went downstairs and watched this elf that was one of Santa Claus' helpers. He brought them some cherries, and a bow, and a pipe and a wreath, and a bowl full of jelly. It was weird."

Weird was how I felt. The child will obviously never make a good poetry critic.

The Mangy Manger Scene

Just when I thought there wasn't a bit of space left anywhere in the house to put out another single Christmas decoration, my son went rummaging through the boxes again, spilling ornament hangers all over the carpet and looking panicky.

"Where's the manger scene? I can't find it," he said. "We have to have the manger scene."

The reason he couldn't find it is that our lumpy, peculiar manger scene was tucked in the top of my closet where I carefully pack it away at the end of each Christmas season.

Ours is one of the most amazing manger scenes in existence. It's home-made, and it looks it. But over the years its importance has grown to equal that of the tree, and no Christmas would be complete without it.

The day we made the manger scene was one of those crummy after-noons every mother dreads, early in December about a dozen years ago.

Outside it was cold and bleak. Inside it was even drearier. Three small people, all with runny noses and just sick enough to be completely cranky, had run out of anything to do but whine and squabble among themselves. The television had lost its charm, and all the toys in the house were pro-nounced boring.

In this sea of discontent, my patience was going down for the third time.

Desperate, I recalled a recipe I had seen, one for rainy day modeling clay. I have forgotten the exact ingredients, but it involved cornstarch and baking soda.

We mixed up a batch, and I gave a mound to each member of my grou-chy little brood. For the first time in several hours harmony reigned as we worked around the dining room table.

My son was the most interested in the project. With a frown of con-centration, he fashioned a smallish figure with four spokes and a strange flat disk on its head.

"What's that dumb looking thing?" asked his oldest sister with all the tact of a 5-year-old.

"That's Baby Jesus," replied my son, poking a hole with a toothpick in the figure's middle. "And that's his tummy button."

"What's that funny thing on his head?"

"That's his little light circle," replied the budding sculptor whose vocabulary didn't yet include the word halo. "I'm going to make Mary and Jesus and Joseph, and they're all going to have little light circles on their heads."

"I want to make Mary and Jesus and Joseph, too," announced my eldest with typical copycat inspiration.

"Me, too," chimed her sister.

So, I suggested that we all work together to create a manger scene.

Everyone was amenable—a very unusual occurrence in those days (these days, too, now that I think of it).

While my son completed Mary, Jesus and Joseph and a manger that looked like a mushroom basket, the girls worked on a donkey, a lamb and a cat. As far as I know, there is no Biblical authority for a cat at the birth of Christ, but at our house you have to expect to find a cat anywhere.

My contribution to the scene was a couple of angels.

As we worked, making suggestions and admiring each other's efforts, the grouchy dispositions vanished. I made hot chocolate and popcorn, and the conversation turned toward cheery anticipation of Christmas. And outside, a weak December sun appeared.

At the end of the afternoon, we put our still-damp figures together. The stable at Bethlehem was never so homey.

Mary and Joseph lean together over the manger, just as you might expect proud parents to hover over their baby. But in this case they lean together because one of Joseph's legs is considerably shorter than the other one. Baby Jesus, his arms and legs outstretched perfectly straight, can't lie in the manger; he has to lie on top of it. He resembles a starfish, complete with tummy button and halo.

The donkey has to be propped on the corner of the manger in order not to topple over, but the best piece is the lamb, who really looks quite a bit like a lamb. The angels are chubbier than the average angel, and one of them reminds me of Jackie Gleason.

We dried our figurines on top of the heater, and sometime between that afternoon and Christmas Eve we painted them.

Now every Christmas my almost-grown children place the manger scene somewhere near the Christmas tree, and someone inevitably recalls the long-ago afternoon of the popcorn and hot chocolate and my son's bright idea.

I hope your holiday memories are happy ones, too. Merry Christmas.

The Season
of the Snoops

"Do your Christmas shopping early, and you'll avoid the rush," go the words to an advertising jingle from Christmas past.

At our house, if you do your Christmas shopping early, all you'll do is guarantee that by Christmas Eve everyone will have found out what you're giving.

'Tis the season to snoop, and I live with a bunch of snoops. When the snoops strike, no closet is safe. Neither are gifts hidden under a bed or in the trunk of an automobile. The Christmas snoops will find them, open them, inspect them and put them back so carefully you never realize you've been tricked until they fail to look surprised on Christmas morning.

The Christmas snoops keep strange hours, working with flashlights and stealthy tread between the witching hour and the dawn's early light. They also work during my office hours. They strike swiftly, leaving few tracks and no fingerprints. They are cunning and thorough.

The Christmas snoops do not respect property. They rummage glee-fully through dresser drawers and in my desk when I'm not at home. They read my bills to see what I've purchased lately and in what colors and sizes.

The Christmas snoops conspire, providing shoulders for each other to stand on in order to see onto top closet shelves. They plot and connive. They also giggle a lot.

The Christmas snoops will call me up at work, disguising their voices and pretending to be telephone surveyors.

"Hello, there. I am a computer, and this is a shopping survey. What are the most important gifts you're giving your children for Christmas this year?" asks the strangely familiar yet unfamiliar voice on the line.

Would I be fooled by that? Almost.

The snoops also snoop on each other—Snoop vs. Snoop. In these cases, the giggles of the pre-Christmas Snoop Season turn to threats and screams of outrage.

"Get out of my room, Dummy. I'm wrapping your stupid Christmas present!"

Or:

"You twerp! You looked in that box on purpose! Now I'm not even going to give it to you."

As the customary victim of the snoop brigade, I have to admit I find these times tremendously gratifying.

Till recently, it appeared that the only way to outsmart the Christmas snoops and maintain the element of surprise was to do my shopping at the last minute, have my gifts wrapped at the store and never let them out of my sight until I put them in the hands of the presentee.

One year I bought all the stocking stuffers early, put them in sealed jars and hid them in the toilet tanks. They found them.

Another year I put them in my safe deposit box at the bank. But I forgot to go get them before the bank closed on Christmas Eve and had to go out and get new ones on the way home. I hid the new ones in the oven. They found them.

One year I wrapped all their gifts in freezer wrap and stashed them in the freezer, labeled "chicken livers," "spinach" and "rutabagas." They found them.

Then there was the year I wrapped their packages and put them under the tree with fake tags on them: To Aunt Lillian, To Uncle Allen.

"Why are you giving Aunt Lillian a Scrabble game?" asked the senior snoop.

"Why are you giving Uncle Allen a model space ship?" asked my snoopy son.

Obviously, they waited until I was out Christmas shopping and opened all the gifts, no matter to whom they were addressed. Curses! Foiled again!

But this year I've discovered that there's more than one way to scoop a snoop. This year I've hit on the best, the safest, the most secure Christmas Present Hiding Place ever.

I don't know why I didn't think of it earlier. It's easy, it's convenient—right in the house—and it'll hold all of my Christmas gifts with room to spare. They'll never find them.

Where is it? Oh, ho, ho, ho. I'll never tell. They read this column, too.

Cats 9, Tree 0

I think that I shall never see
Another Lawson Christmas tree.

—not by Joyce Kilmer

Our house is decorated with greenery and redery. The mantels have Chrismas balls and garlands, the dining table has red candles, and the stockings are hung by the chimney with care.

But there's no tree.

Right away, I hear you say, "Un-American!"

Possibly. But I can explain.

Remember our four cats? Let me refresh you. Max is the yellow one, 16 years old and former backyard-fence fighter. Max is the one whose "Meow" has always sounded more like "Wow."

Puds is a dainty calico, about eight years old. Puds is not a friendly feline. She doesn't like anyone but me, and she doesn't like me much.

Puddin' is yellow and white, about a year old and huge. He has lots of muscles—mostly between his ears—and he's affectionate. His favorite household appliance is the can opener.

Spike is the little black and white cat who visits all our neighbors within a four-block radius. Now and then she comes home for a brief visit.

Last Christmas, before we became wiser, we dragged in a ceiling-high Christmas tree and set it up in the living room. While we were in the attic getting out the Christmas decorations, we heard a rustle and a swish and a crash.

Sure enough, we arrived on the scene to find the tree lying on its side. Four cats sat nearby, busily washing various parts of their anatomies. There was a great deal of very audible purring. What an innocent scene.

We set the tree back up, vacuumed up the loose needles from the carpet, put the cats outside and decorated the tree.

Of course, as soon as someone opened the door, the cats came tumbling back in. By that time, we were all busy with other things and had forgotten the threat to the tree.

It was a matter of just a few moments before we heard the ominous noise.

There is no other noise quite like that of a falling Christmas tree. First there's the rustle of quaking branches. Then there's that slow, agonizing swish during which you realize what's happening and that it's too late to stop it. Then there's the crash, accompanied by the tinkle of dangling lights and ornaments and the smashing of broken ones.

We ran to the living room. There, tangled guiltily among the branches and the wires, were Puddin' and Spike.

We put the two culprits outside in the cold, righted the tree and its decorations, swept up the broken glass and vacuumed up the scattered needles.

Night fell. Because Max is so old, he sleeps indoors. Max wouldn't bother the tree, I reasoned. He's too arthritic and too angelic. My mistake.

Just at bedtime I heard the ominous rustle and swish. And Max's voice came wafting on the midnight air, a prolonged "Wowww"—apparently a feline version of "Timberrrr."

I arrived in the den in time to see him scrambling frantically for a clawhold among the highest branches as the falling tree swept him a wide arc.

He landed with a thump and a yowl and picked his way through the branches, growling furiously.

I put Max in the basement and righted the tree, which was taking on a bedraggled appearance by this time. I picked up the pieces of broken ornaments and vacuumed up the needles from the carpet.

For reasons of limited column space, I will skip over the next five times the cats felled the tree. By Christmas morning, the tree had a definite battle-weary look—a most un-spruce looking spruce. Most of its ornaments were gone. Few of the lights still burned. The tinsel appeared to have been scrambled.

The final tree toppling—the ninth—occurred during supper one night during the week after Christmas. This time it was Puds who sailed down in a shower of needles, lights and ornaments.

We gave up, took off what was left of the decorations and dragged the tree outside.

This year, when the subject of a tree came up, my son expressed the sentiments of the whole family. He said, "I just don't want to go through it again."

'Twas the Day After . . .

' Twas the day after Christmas and all through the house rang the wail of the post-Christmas child:

"There's nothing to do."

For nearly two decades now, those words have marked the arrival of every Dec. 26. They're as traditional as "Silent Night" is on Dec. 25.

Santa has come and gone. The presents have been opened and examined, and all the "Wows" have faded.

The unstuffed stockings hang forlorn and empty, and the candy is all eaten up.

The turkey that was golden and aromatic has been reduced to a few cold shreds on a carcass; the cats have lapped up the last of the gravy; and there's a general hue and cry for hamburgers for supper—"or anything but turkey, Mom."

The tree spreads its branches over a living room shambles that resembles Fifth Avenue after a ticker tape parade. Bits of wrapping paper and tatters of ribbon festoon every horizontal surface.

After months of anticipation, all closets are open, all secrets have been revealed.

And only crumbs remain in the cookie tins.

Everyone agrees it was a great Christmas, probably the best ever. The new tapes are all terrific; the sweaters are the right color; the fluorescent socks and sweatshirts all fit; and the designer jeans (are we ever going to be through with designer jeans?) are just the thing.

The checks that Grandma sent with her gifts were a delightful surprise, and for once Great Aunt Maggie sent nightshirts that no one would rather be dead than be seen in.

The jumble of boxes and giftwrap has been carefully sifted, and that famous Christmas afternoon question, "Is this all?" has been asked and answered in the affirmative.

A tired but happy trio at last trooped off to bed on Christmas night, every electronic and fashion wish having become reality.

And now it's Dec. 26, and, "There's nothing to do."

For the first decade or so, I felt compelled to try to find an answer for "There's nothing to do."

As the long hours of Dec. 26 wore on, I racked my brain for antidotes to the boredom. So, it is from experience that I can attest the following suggestions are futile and will avail you nothing:

"Why don't you get all your presents from under the tree and put them in your room?"

("Yuck. I don't wanna.")

"Why don't you be a good little elf and pick up all the wrapping paper and put it in the trash container?"

("Get someone else. I cleaned up the breakfast dishes, remember?")

"Why don't we make some hot chocolate and pop popcorn and play Trivial Pursuit?"

("There isn't any milk, and besides I'm tired of trivia.")

"Why don't you sit down with your new stationery and write your thank you notes?"

("Aw, gee, Mom, do we havta write thank you notes?")

"Why don't you be a good little elf and feed the cats?"

("The cats got into the turkey dressing. They aren't hungry anymore.")

"Why don't you listen to your new records (tapes, radio, etc.)?"

("Don't wanna.")

"Why don't you sit down and plan your New Year's resolutions?"

("Yuck.")

"Why don't you see what's on TV?"

("There's nothing but icky soap operas.")

"Why don't you go down the street and see what John got for Christmas?"

("I did that yesterday. Besides, his stupid cousins are still there.")

This can go on as long as you're willing to offer suggestions.

But a few years ago I discovered the single, the only, the surefire successful response to "There's nothing to do."

Here it is:

Teens: "There's nothing to do."

Mom: "Here are the car keys, and the tank is full of gas. Why don't you go somewhere until suppertime?"

Teens (all smiles; it's Christmas again): "Terrif! See ya later, Mom."

Door slams. Peace on earth.

Up A Tree: My Life with Cats
(Or, When I Said I Wanted a Fur,
This Wasn't What I Had in Mind)

Sometimes it seems that our cats own the house and just let us live there. Five cats were the subjects of the columns that follow: Stumpy and Max, both of whom lived with us many years before going to that Great Hunting Ground in the Sky; Puddin', who won our hearts in our few short months together; and the current managers of the household, Half 'n' Half (otherwise known as Puds) and Spike.

I started to name this chapter Torn Curtain. Clawed Furniture seemed appropriate, too. But Up a Tree says it best, since that's where I often feel I am.

Cats and More Cats

Kittens, kittens, a whole new litter of kittens. Just what I've always wanted.

To tell the truth, we viewed the arrival of this particular batch of kitties with some anticipation. They were bound to be cute, because their mother is an exceptionally amusing member of our household.

A product of the humane society, she bears the name Half 'n' Half because she was said to be half Persian and half something else. I suspect she's mostly something else, since she neither looks nor speaks Persian. However, she is such a really charming little cat that we expect great things of her offspring.

Of course, it's reasonable to assume that at least some of the kits will take after their pa, who was a traveling man. We never met him, although we were made painfully aware of his presence in our back yard about two months ago. There are few things that sound or smell worse than an amorous tomcat.

Shortly after his visit, it was discovered that Half 'n' Half was in kit. This, I have been told, is the delicate term used by cat fanciers to describe the condition of a pregnant feline.

Not at all dismayed by the prospect of becoming an unwed mother, Half 'n' Half continued her usual routine during the early weeks of her pregnancy—walking on all of us in our beds during the wee hours of the morning, kneading her claws in our shoulders, hopping into our plates during meals and stalking bits of fluff under the furniture.

But as her size increased, Half 'n' Half began napping more often and bouncing less.

She also began nibbling my houseplants. Suspecting that she might be suffering from a vitamin deficiency, I enriched her diet with chopped liver and raw eggs. She responded by consuming an entire potted palm (a small one) one night, leaving only the stem. This evidently satisfied her craving for vegetables. Thereafter, she left the houseplants alone.

Then came the beginning of her search for the place to have the kittens. Ponderously—by this time, she was enormous—she examined every dark and secluded nook in the house. She was here, there and all over, sniffing and scratching in closets and dresser drawers, peering into cabinets, sizing up space under the beds. Then she made a mistake. She settled upon the clothes dryer one day, hopped in and curled up happily.

Unfortunately, she went unnoticed, and the first hint I had that Half 'n' Half had selected the dryer was a funny sounding "Thunk! Thunk!" as I dried a load of clothes. When I opened the door to find out what all the noise was about, she leaped out, looking not only warm and astonished but also somewhat fluff dried. After that, she left the dryer alone.

When the kittens finally came, she had them in a cardboard box set out for that purpose behind the bookcases in the den. Throughout her pregnancy, she had refused to consider the box at all, hopping out with tail twitching angrily when I attempted to show her what a nice box it was. After that, the box was the last place I would have expected her to choose, which is probably why she chose it.

The kits arrived one afternoon while I was at the grocery store, and no one was home. The first indication we had of their presence was Half 'n' Half's newly streamlined figure, which we noticed when she appeared in the kitchen for supper.

Now we are engaged in that time-honored pursuit of cat owners, trying to find homes for the babies.

Anybody want a kitten?

Kittens Into Cats

You can always tell when a kitten is making the transition from kitten-hood to cathood by the way it begins turning up its nose at the foods you serve it.

Kittens will eat anything—from cold oatmeal to canned peach juice. They delight in leftovers, growing sleek on the leavings of your breakfast plate, and purr merrily as they lap up drops of tomato juice from your kitchen floor.

Kittens are born recognizing the sound of the electric can opener. As soon as it can walk, a kitten will fall all over itself rushing to the kitchen anytime it hears the magic noise, just in case a little snack may be in the offing.

We had a litter of kittens once that demolished a loaf of bread. They chewed the middles out of each slice but left the crusts—just as certain small children of my acquaintance used to do. Then they moved on and were into the potato chips when I found them.

I once surprised a kitten crouched in my kitchen sink with one paw down the food disposer, trying to snare a piece of lettuce.

You'd think that a kitten who behaved in this manner was starving. However, only five minutes earlier the same kitten had licked clean a soup bowl full of leftover beef stew. His little sides were bulging as he desper-ately fished for the lettuce leaf in the disposer.

Kittens thrive on dry catfood and will gnaw their way through the cardboard box to get to it, if you're not handily available to serve it up in their bowl.

Kittens are simply non-stop eaters.

But suddenly one day, your voracious kitten becomes a finicky, picky cat. It views the contents of its foodbowl with disdain, no matter what you put in it. It meows pitifully as it gazes from filled foodbowl to you and back again with big, sad eyes. It swears it hasn't had a thing to eat in three weeks.

You fall into the trap. You worry that the kitten is sick. You croon sweet nothings and attempt to lure it with tempting tidbits. You chop up fresh liver for the kitten. The kitten sniffs it with little interest and begins to wash its paws.

You get out the raw chicken you were going to fry for supper and cut off kitty-bite-sized pieces. The kitten continues washing. You decide to call the vet.

But as you're looking up the number in the phone book, the kitten leaps to the top of the refrigerator, spills a box of grapenuts flakes and begins crunching away.

Furiously, you fling the kitten into the back yard where he soon hunts up a mouse and a chipmunk, gobbles them down and leaves the gory remains on your doormat for you to clean up.

Your kitten has become a cat.

I'm convinced the transition comes about when they learn to read. Oh, yes, kittens learn to read at about six months of age.

The kitten who delighted in slurping up a whole can of cheap, generic catfood suddenly becomes suspicious, checking the price on the top of the can before settling down to dine.

If the price is high enough to meet the cat's standards, all is well. But none of your el cheapo brands anymore, please. And forget the dry food.

Cats also read the fine print on labels. I once discovered a cat in my kitchen squinting at a can of cheap catfood I had foolishly bought and left out on the counter. He was reading the list of ingredients. I read it, too. It said, among other things, "filler." Never again would that cat eat that brand of cat food.

After a cat learns to read, the name of the catfood becomes a matter of immense importance to the cat. Cans labeled Gourmet Treat, Liver in Creamed Gravy, Chicken and Sauce, Seafood Supper, Western Menu or Omelet and Cheese are usually acceptable.

But don't push your luck. The cat that ravaged a can of Seafood Supper last week wants nothing but Western Menu this week. Next week he'll demand Sliced Beef in Cream. Cats like variety.

I have always wondered what you do when you come to the absolute end of new flavors for your finicky cat to sample. Anticipating this dilemma, I am considering creating fake labels to paste onto cheap cans of catfood.

I'll name them Mouse in Sauce, Chipmunk in Gravy, Rat Remoulade. I may put in a bird line—Blue Jay, Barn Swallow, Canary Cakes and Parakeet Treat.

The only alternative solution I can think of is to give the cats away and get a dog.

My Friend Stumpy

Stumpy is a yellow striped cat with a white bib, round green eyes, an ingratiating manner—and no tail. He lost his tail in what must have been a gruesome accident, because when he was found the skin and fur had been wrenched off in a jagged tear, leaving the bone protruding several inches. He had no other injuries—just the mangled tail.

I can't imagine how it could have happened. The absence of other injuries could mean that it was done intentionally. There are people who delight in harming small animals, just as there are people who delight in harming small children. I hope there is a special hell set aside for both groups.

I prefer to think that Stumpy may have backed into a lawnmower or stuck his tail into an electric fan to see what would happen.

At any rate, some kind people found him and took him to the vet where he became a charity case.

When I first saw him, he was curled into a despondent ball in his cage.

"We're trying to find a home for him," I was told. "But no one seems to want an injured cat."

And so, of course, Stumpy came home to live with us. He cowered in a corner of the porch for a couple of days, until he decided he was in a safe place, after which he set about to investigate his new home and make friends with his new family.

Surgery was required later because the injured tail refused to heal. Our vet did a fine job, and Stumpy now has just about an inch of tail, covered with a nice growth of fur. There is only the smallest scar at the very end.

Because of his tailless state, Stumpy cannot pursue all of the amusements of cats. He cannot climb high into a tree because he lacks the balance that a tail affords when tiptoeing on the highest branches.

If he falls, he cannot right himself and land feet-first as cats are known to be able to do.

When stalking a mouse or squirrel, he cannot twitch just the veriest tip of his tail, as all cats do when stalking. However, when he is angry, the stump of his tail twitches furiously.

But he can purr, and does frequently—the loudest I've ever known any grown cat to purr. And he listens when I talk to him, answering with a small meow when he thinks it's appropriate.

He eats prodigious amounts and is not at all persnickety. Broccoli suits him just fine, and he is extremely fond of vanilla ice cream with chocolate sauce.

If I am reading and he wants my attention, he hops onto my lap and stands on the book until I give up and put it down.

Occasionally, he regresses into kittenhood, hopping sideways, turning somersaults and chasing—well, chasing where his tail ought to be.

Maybe it's because he was injured and homeless that I am so partial to Stumpy. Even without a tail, he is a beautiful cat. And he has proven to be a gentle and entertaining friend.

A Long Winter's Nap

From ghoulies and ghosties and long-leggety beasties and things that go bump in the night, Good Lord, deliver us.—Scottish prayer.

During the recent arctic storm, while our trees creaked and squeaked beneath their coatings of ice, and the branches popping off the pines sounded like rifles being fired outside the windows, I had occasion to think of things that go bump in the night.

Usually our house is filled with nighttime noises. The refrigerator hums in the kitchen, the furnace blower goes on and off, the hot water heater whines mysteriously in the basement and the house makes its own occasional noises—all familiar, soothing and sleep inducing.

But on this night the storm had cut off the power that fuels these night-time activities.

No furnace-refrigerator-water heater noises cajoled Morpheus to his nightly visit. Inside the house it was icy cold and deadly quiet, magnifying the eerie noises outdoors.

It was an uncomfortable silence, the sort of total silence that demands you listen to it. I listened and wondered if the silence bothered the children as much as it was bothering me. It was. It was disturbing the cats, too, as I was shortly to find out.

At our house, when something goes bump in the night it is likely to be a child or a short-leggety beastie of the feline variety. I have grown accustomed to being thumped awake in the wee, dark hours, to the extent that even in my groggiest state I can tell which one of them is responsible for the awakening.

Among us, there is one staunch, brave soul. If Gabriel blows his horn in the middle of the night, we will have to wake up my older daughter to meet her Maker. She sleeps serenely through emergencies, disasters and thunderstorms. But she apparently does not sleep through icy silences.

Only a few minutes after we turned out the lights, I heard the gentle tread of bare feet and felt the covers on the far side of the bed being turned back. With a thud and a snuggle, Ghostie Number One wedged an ancient stuffed tiger—her bedtime companion of almost 17 years—between us. Without a word, she yawned and pulled off all my covers, settling in and tucking them snugly around herself. I fumbled for the edge of the blanket and pulled a corner of it back around me.

More silence.

Then more quiet footsteps. Ghostie Number Two padded into the room. "Move over, Mama," she demanded, backing under the covers without ceremony and shoving me into her sister on the other side.

More silence, punctuated by rhythmic breathing. Then a heavy branch cracked and crashed to the ground, thudding on the roof and brushing the window.

This brought Beasties One and Two to the scene.

Puds, our smallest cat, walks with a velvet tread. The first notice of her arrival was, as always, a gentle thud on my feet. She curled up and began to purr musically.

Things are different with Max. Max is huge, arthritic and lumbering, a sort of Henry the Eighth among cats. His purr reminds me of a chain saw with a rusty spark plug. I could hear his purr coming down the hall and braced myself. Max always pauses in the doorway, lines up his jump with all the concentration of an Olympic pole vaulter, and leaps onto my head. He made a perfect four-point landing and marched up and down my back, surveying the situation and rumbling majestically.

Finding my pillow to his liking, he made a few tight circles and curled up with his fluffy back against my nose. In order to continue breathing, I moved over and gave him the middle of the pillow.

Next to arrive was Stumpy, our beastie with the truncated tail who is under the delusion that he owns us all, including the house and my bed.

Stumpy hopped onto the bedside table, a king-on-the-mountain vantage point from which to challenge Max for the pillow. Stumpy and Max have frequent territorial disputes that would wake the dead. They simply cannot settle anything in gentlemanly fashion.

Following a ferocious debate, Stumpy slunk to the foot of the bed, paused to growl at the stuffed tiger, and draped himself sulkily over the far corner.

By this time, the silence was broken by lots of breathing. Enter Ghostie Number Three, my son, dragging his blanket behind him and carrying his pillow. Usually the last to arrive, he has learned to bring his own bedding because the floor is the only spot left unclaimed.

Thus did the ghosties and short-legged beasties pass the long night. No one got much sleep, but it certainly was cozy.

Home From the Hills

Our hunter came home from the neighborhood hills this weekend—
lacerated, bloody and battle worn.

Max the Magnificent, the fearless forager, the warrior cat, was hud-
dled by the door Sunday night, a miserable bundle of tattered, bloody,
yellow fur.

I don't know whether he tangled with a dog or another cat, but for the
first time in his long life it appeared that whatever he battled got the best
of him.

As I write, he is languishing in the animal hospital, recovering from what
I hope will be the final fight in a lifetime of combat.

Max is full of years. Arthritis has leadened his gait. Deafness has dulled
his awareness. He chases no more butterflies, and the neighbors' dogs tres-
pass in his food dish with impunity. Even the pesky mockingbirds rarely
bother to taunt him.

An increasing measure of his time is spent dozing in my rose bed. Sunshine feels good on old bones. But age has not dimmed his fighting spirit.
His head is bloody but unbowed.

There is an element of tact that must be brought to bear in dealing with
the aging. For this reason, until now, I have been reluctant to confine Max
to the house. He has always been an outdoor man, roaming the fields by
day and night, proudly bringing home the mangled remains of squirrels,
rabbits, mice and an occasional rat. These trophies he always deposited on
the doormat for us to find—concrete evidence of his prowess.

But in recent months, his horizons have narrowed; the boundaries of
our yard have begun to mark the perimeters of his roaming.

My first instinct, after almost tripping over his inert form in the dark-
ened carport, was to pick him up and carry him into the house. But an old
cat has his pride, and he lurched to his feet and back away from my outstretched hands.

So I opened the door and held it for him, and he dragged himself into
the house and to his favorite indoor resting spot under the dining room

table. He purred a feeble rumble upon reaching his haven of retreat, stag-
gered in the circle that is the instinct of cats and sank down wearily on the
carpet, his sides heaving.

He spent the night there, declining food and water. He slept so deeply
that he didn't rouse when I visited him several times during the dark hours.

Next morning, he limped into the kitchen when he saw me turn on the
light to make morning coffee.

As I heated water, he went to the glass-paned back door and looked
out, and in a few moments I heard the low, gutteral growl of cat hate. An
interloper, one of the neighborhood toms—a lean, muscled, gray-striped
athlete who has been one of Max's regular adversaries—was sitting in the
curve of his tail on our deck. To add insult to the injury of his presence,
the intruder was calmly washing his ears.

There was blood in Max's eye as he demanded that I open the door.
(Max has always requested out in English: "Let Meowt," he says.) But I
imagined the outcome of the fight, with my old cat in his present state,
and I left the door closed. Thwarted, he protested loudly, so I diverted him
with a breakfast of his favorite Tuna Treat.

We traveled to the vet with Max in the red cardboard cat carrier we use
in such emergencies. He hates even the sight of the carrier, but Max un-
confined in a moving automobile is unsafe at any speed. He races in circles, clawing anyone in his path, tearing up the upholstery and hurling
insults at the world in tones that would stun a banshee.

Max hates the whole business of riding to the vet. The only battle he
ever lost was with a car that ran over him. He emerged from under the
wheels with two broken legs and one of his nine lives used up, and he's
never forgiven the insult.

But this morning he didn't fight being placed in the carrier—a measure
of his injuries. He rode to the hospital peering at me through the little air
holes and meekly mewing his disgust. (And I have seen the day Max would
shred an entire cardboard carrier between our house and the vet's office.
He is not over-fond of vets.)

He will return home in a day or two, and I hope we can make the house
an interesting enough retreat for a retired warrior. But in any event, he will
have to adjust.

From now on, Max is a house cat.

Remembering Max

The flat rock at the back of the flower bed is almost hidden now beneath a drift of dead leaves.

The brittle stalks of summer's zinnias rattle in the cold wind, and overhead the branches of the sweetgum tree are sharply outlined against the gray sky.

Still, the small black and white cat goes each late afternoon to the low wall that borders the garden. Her ritual is always the same. Hopping to the wall, she settles into a crouch, tucking her paws beneath her until she is a compact bundle wrapped snugly within the circle of her tail.

Then, for an hour or so, she watches the rock with an intense, secret gaze.

"Look, Mom," says my son. "Spike is visiting Max's grave again. You'd think she would have forgotten by now."

Together we look through the kitchen window, both remembering Max and wondering whether memories are stirring between Spike's pointed ears.

Do cats think? Do they remember? Do they grieve? My son believes they do.

It has been more than two months since Max died. His death was not unexpected; his 17 years were more than most cats are allotted, and they were 17 years of bloody combat. If the neighborhood's tomcats have forgotten Max, they need only take a look at their scars to remember.

I had expected Max to die on the field of battle, or of wounds following one of his fierce encounters. Instead, he toppled peacefully onto his side one balmy October evening as he was washing up after a tuna fish supper. In the instant it took me to fly down the steps and pick him up, he was gone.

Max was an orange tabby, born in a cardboard box in our den the same year my son was born. They grew up together, and Max was the only cat I ever knew who tolerated being pulled around the yard in a red wagon. He sat on the sidelines during small-fry football games and patiently endured my daughters' tea parties with a damask napkin tied around his huge neck.

But at night, he prowled the neighborhood, looking for a fight and usually finding one. His subsequent recovery at the animal hospital was always expensive.

Max moved with us from Hawkinsville to Dublin and to two homes in Macon, hastening each time to establish himself as lord of the new neighborhood.

In all his days, he was fond of only five things: cat fights, food, napping at the foot of my bed, the humans with whom he lived, and the cats who shared our household with him.

He was not tolerant of people outside the family; he viewed all strange cats as The Enemy; and he purely hated dogs.

Max's sidekick for many years was a tailless yellow and white cat we named Stumpy. After Stumpy died, Max spent his days alone until two years ago when Spike joined the household as a kitten.

By that time, Max was creaky with arthritis. But even worse, he was becoming deaf, and in his last days it was obvious that he was puzzled. His humans would look at him and move their lips, but there was no sound. Why had we quit talking to him? He would follow us around the house, weaving between our feet, meowing piteously for an answering noise.

And so, a ritual began. As often as possible, one of us would pick Max up, holding his head against our throats and talking to him so that he could feel the vibrations of a voice. And he would purr loudly on these occasions, snuggling up and kneading his huge claws painfully into our shoulders.

As Max became increasingly infirm, we tried keeping him indoors for his own safety. But it was useless. From early morning to far past bedtime, he howled with rage, shredding drapes, mauling furniture and hurling himself against the glass door, outside of which his territory lay unpatrolled.

After a week of this, I gave up and let him out, and was glad to note that he no longer ranged far afield in search of opponents. He spent his days curled in the backyard flower bed, viewing the antics of the bouncy new kitten.

Before long, they had become friends, sharing a foodbowl and purring together in the sunshine.

My son buried Max behind the flowers in the garden and marked the spot with a large rock. Spike sat nearby and watched the funeral with green-eyed curiosity. From that day to this, Spike has paid a daily visit to the spot. And, we wonder, is Spike remembering? Is she thinking?

And if so, what?

Train Up a Cat . . .

During our current spate of wintry weather, I've discovered yet another reason why cats are useful.

In my decades of cat ownership, I've become a zealous student of the utilitarian properties of cats. (I can't recall any of them at the moment, but surely they will occur to me as I continue to write.)

Anyway, in the cold, dreary days that have followed our 0-degree Christmas, I have made a new and delightful discovery in the area of cat-usefulness: A curled-up cat is very warm and is thus useful.

If you can pursuade your cat to drape his furry body over your cold feet while you watch television, you will soon begin—for the first time in weeks—to regain feeling in your toes.

Once your feet begin to warm up, the rest of you will start to thaw in an amazingly short time.

You will save energy and reduce your heating bills.

And there is something cozy and friendly about the subtle vibrations of a cat purring on your feet.

Of course, you may have a problem pursuading the cat that on your feet is where he wants to be.

Just as soon as you decide you want a cat to serve as a miniature afghan, the cat will decide he wants to go outside and chase birds. Or sit in front of the refrigerator and howl for a snack. Or go anywhere except where you want him.

So, you must be resourceful.

One way to entice a cat to curl up on your feet is to smear catfood around and between your toes. You may find the mushy sensation of ground chicken parts revolting at first, but as your feet begin to toast beneath the snacking cat, you'll decide the ultimate benefits far outweigh the initial discomfort.

You need to remember also that it's possible (cats being carnivorous) that your toes will begin disappearing along with the catfood. You'll want to take steps to prevent this if at all possible.

Another plan is to tie the warm cat to your cold feet with a stout rope or cord.

A drawback to this method is that it is difficult to secure the cat's co-operation while you tie the knots. The typical cat will squirm impatiently and very shortly begin to claw and bite.

Wearing heavy hunting boots will reduce the number and depth of tooth and claw lacerations, but I can almost hear you arguing that heavy hunting boots are not your choice of footwear for comfortable television viewing.

Well, don't be so picky-picky. You can't have everything.

Another method is to watch television programs that interest cats. That way, the enthralled cat will forget he's sitting on your feet while he gazes raptly into the action on the screen. This will necessitate your giving up "60 Minutes" and "M*A*S*H" reruns, since cats prefer shows that involve food. Check your TV schedule for reruns of the Mouseketeers, tune in to a Tweety Bird cartoon or spin the dial until you happen upon a Purina commercial.

But remember that cats have a short attention span. Your cat will want you to get up every few minutes to switch channels, and each time you do, you'll have to repersuade the cat to get back on your feet.

Don't become discouraged. Extensive research I conducted yesterday during my lunch hour turned up documented cases that show a few cats have actually been trained to warm their owners' feet upon command.

For instance, during the bitter Siberian Blizzard of 1883, a salt miner in the town of Myakit trained his cat to hop onto his feet at the command "Smof," which is Russian for foot.

And in Antlers, Utah, during the famous Comanche Uprising of '47 (with which I'm sure you're all familiar, so I won't go into the historical details), members of the Seventh Cavalry used trained wildcats to warm their feet prior to riding into battle.

But these cases are rare. And if you'll look in the yellow pages, you'll notice a general absence of obedience schools for cats.

Still, in view of their energy-saving properties, you may want to consider adopting several cats as warm and friendly footwarmers for each member of your family.

Just remember, sitting around training the family cats as footwarmers is a good way to promote togetherness in the home.

And if you reverse the process, keeping the cats off your feet in summer, you will save on air conditioning.

When Dinosaurs Roamed
(Or, Yes, Dear,
Even Mom Had a Childhood)

When my son was very young, he asked, "Mama, when you were little were dinosaurs wild like lions and tigers, or did people have them for pets?"

I told him the truth, of course, that by the time I was born most dinosaurs had been domesticated.

Stories from my childhood have been favorites of my children. And they have provided me with material for many columns—even though I never did have a pet dinosaur.

Easter Memories

My maternal grandfather died in Emory University Hospital on a sunny April afternoon shortly after my seventh birthday. Far too early, at the age of just 63, he lost his battle with a failing heart, and I lost my best friend.

He was blessed with an enormous intellectual capacity, a sparkling sense of humor and a lively curiosity about things in nature and science. His legacy to me is a crowd of happy memories.

The flowering of the azaleas and dogwoods and the spring song of the wood thrushes always remind me of him, but I think of him in all seasons.

There were winter nights when I would sit in his lap and investigate his shirt pocket and suspenders while he worked calculus problems for his own entertainment and drew cartoons for mine. He had graduated from Georgia Tech as a mechanical engineer while still in his teens, and he said the calculus helped him keep his mind stretched. In between calculus problems, he would draw cartoons in which a small girl figured prominently. I was fascinated.

On summer nights, we would sit on the front porch. If I were reasonably quiet while he listened to the news on the radio, he would afterwards fashion a matchbox with a string harness to be pulled around the floor by one of the fat green June bugs that darted around the porch light. The biggest June bug could even fly with its tiny "car" attached. At bedtime, he would carefully unharness the bug, which, he told me, would fly home to tell its family of its exciting adventure with the matchbox.

Summertime meant collecting the castoff skins of July flies that clung with dried brown legs to the bark of pine trees in the back yard. We investigated the tiny split in the back of each skin, and he would tell me about the beautiful green bug that had emerged and stretched its wings.

He always listened with gravity to my ideas and treated the projects of a small child with respect. Once, at my suggestion, we dug a trench under the blackgum tree and planted a row of marbles. I watered them daily, but no marble trees grew. We decided those marbles were probably the wrong kind for planting and finally dug them back up again and planted zinnias instead. The zinnias proved much more satisfactory.

At Thanksgiving, the family—aunts, uncles and cousins—gathered in my grandmother's dining room for the feast. My grandfather carved the turkey. One Thanksgiving, the drop leaf of the table gave way, and the turkey—dressing, gravy and all—fell into his lap. He said a whole string of interesting new words when that happened. A few days later, when I parroted some of the words he had used, he tried, but failed, to be stern and said something I didn't understand about little pitchers and big ears.

Christmas was another memorable season. There was always something fun going on when my grandfather was around. I awoke one Christmas morning to find that during the night, the pear tree in the front yard had produced half a dozen oranges and grapefruit. In my excitement, I failed to notice that they were tied onto the branches with string. It was years later before I was told of my grandfather's midnight visit to decorate the pear tree.

One spring, we purloined a blossom from one of my grandmother's prized Easter lilies and spent a scientific hour or so taking it apart and examining the silky white petals, the pistil and the dusty yellow stamens under a magnifying glass.

Easter was the time of the great egg dyeing, a ritual he and I enjoyed annually. I think of him whenever I eat a hard-boiled egg.

He would arrive home early from his office with a grocery sack full of eggs in cartons and a few boxes of egg dye. I would prance around the kitchen, much excited and probably getting in the way, while he took care of the mundane task of boiling the eggs.

My favorite part was putting the teaspoon of vinegar on the colored pellet in the bottom of the cup and watching it dissolve. That was my job. His was pouring in the hot water from the teakettle after I melted the pellets. I was always all for checking the eggs immediately to see how they were coming along in the dye, so he would tell me a story as a diversion while we waited.

He enjoyed a personal rapport with the Easter Bunny, who would always let him know what time he would be hopping by to hide eggs. My grandfather would consult his pocket watch and go outside for a little while, then come back in to say he had just spoken with E. Bunny and learned that numerous eggs were hidden in the front yard. While hunting, I failed to notice that they looked much like the eggs we had dyed a few days earlier.

Easter was always the best time of all.

An Unauthorized Tour

The sanctuary door closed softly behind the 6-year-old girl, swallowing up the noise of the city street.

She stood for a moment, peering through the dimness to the altar dominated by a white marble Christ on a huge cross.

Only the muffled hum of Christmas traffic could be heard through the cathedral's stone walls.

The little girl peered around warily, her hand still on the door. Unless someone was praying at one of the side altars, she was alone. She could spend about 10 minutes, and if she ran home no one would notice she was later than usual.

Timidly she advanced down the marble-floored center aisle, trying to keep her tiptoed footsteps from echoing too loudly.

She wondered what would happen if she were found here. She had already decided to say she was making a visit. The nuns always advocated making a visit to Jesus, who lived in the church and who got lonely when children didn't come to see him.

She walked straight to the altar rail and genuflected, crossing herself carefully as the nuns had taught her to do. Then she turned and continued to the side altar where the Advent wreath stood.

There she knelt and folded her hands under her chin, her fingertips pointed toward heaven, her back straight. God liked fingers to be pointed upward like a steeple, the nuns said, and sloppy posture meant sloppy prayers.

Having properly composed herself, the little girl turned her full attention to the Advent wreath. It was beautiful. The three purple candles and one pink one stood tall in the greenery, and, gleaming in the dimness, a wide satin bow—a lavender one—curled and curved and draped almost to the floor.

The wreath was even more beautiful up close than it had been from afar earlier that day when she had attended the first Advent services with her classmates.

In rows they had knelt, shepherded by watchful nuns who discouraged inattentiveness with stern looks and raps on the knuckles for major offenders.

Heads bowed, the children had answered Father McDonough in unison with the words to the litany they had practiced all week: "Christ the Light of the World, have mercy upon us and forgive us our sins."

At the end of the service, Father McDonough, flanked by altar boys and using the slim taper, lighted one of the purple candles in the Advent wreath.

That was when the little girl forgot where she was and stood up. Because the eighth graders sat in the front and the first graders in the back, she had not been able to see over the heads of her taller schoolmates. In a moment of forgetfulness, she stood up to have a better view of the candle-lighting and was mortified to be snatched back down by the hem of her dress—right in front of everyone—by Sister Mary Elizabeth, who frowned hard and shook her finger.

It was horribly embarrassing, and the little girl felt her face burning. What was worse, she hadn't gotten a clear view of the lighting of the Advent candle, and now it would be a whole week before it happened again. That was when she decided to come back after school.

Now that she was alone, kneeling directly in front of the wreath, she could see the black wick of the one candle that had been lighted. Father had explained that one candle would be lighted each week until Christmas, the birthday of the Christ Child. Advent was a time of waiting, he said, waiting for Christ's coming into the world. That was more important, he added, than Santa Claus and getting presents.

The little girl found that to be a difficult concept. The promise of all those presents under the tree made her heart beat faster in a way that the Nativity story just did not. Kneeling before the altar, she resolved to try harder to become more excited about Jesus' birthday and less so about getting presents.

She took a last look at the Advent wreath. It was almost time to go. Feeling bolder now that she had accomplished her mission, the little girl allowed her gaze to travel upward, past the sorrowful face of the Blessed Mother and past the stained glass windows through which the sun poured light in shafts of multicolored splendor. She looked up and up—straight up so that she had to open her mouth—to where the stone walls soared and curved into the apex of the Gothic ceiling far overhead. She had never inspected the ceiling before.

Then she took a few moments to walk around the church, looking into the faces of each of the statues. Saint Joseph, holding his white lilies, was barefooted. With one finger, she touched one of his toes. Then she stood for a moment watching the votive candles flicker in their red glass cups before the Sacred Heart.

With her curiosity thoroughly satisfied, she tiptoed to the heavy, bronze-belted wooden door and let herself back outside again.

All this took place many Advents ago. Still, she never sees an Advent wreath that she doesn't recall the day when she stood up in church to see the lighting of the Advent candle. And then she always thinks, still with some degree of satisfaction, of her unauthorized tour of the cathedral.

A Visit from Aunt Agatha

My mother caught me just as I ran through the front door. Her eyes had a mysterious twinkle.

Aunt Agatha from Hahira had come for a Christmas visit, she said, for the afternoon.

My heart sank. At the age of 10, the thought of entertaining an ancient aunt filled me with gloom. And I had been expecting a visit from Uncle Bobby, who was bringing his new model airplane.

"Who is Aunt Agatha?" I asked. My family had numerous elderly aunts; keeping up with them was not one of my priorities.

"You've probably just forgotten her," said Mother. "She doesn't get around much, and she's very old. Go and speak to her, and don't be shy. She's warming up by the fireplace in the den."

With all the speed of a sloth, I presented myself to Aunt Agatha. A sterner looking old crone never drew breath.

Swathed in afghans and a white lace cap, she had wildly curling hair that stood out like little springs around her ears. Black crocheted mitts were tied at her wrists with satin ribbons. She clutched a knobby walking stick.

"Come closer, child," she croaked froggily as I cringed by the door. "Let me have a good look at you."

Reluctantly, I advanced a few steps. Her clothes smelled old, like a cedar chest. Upon closer inspection, I thought there was something vaguely familiar about her, especially around the nose and mouth. She bore a strong resemblance to someone I knew, but I couldn't decide who it was.

She gave me a piercing look from under a pair of very shaggy eyebrows.

"Hah!" she exclaimed loudly, and I jumped with fright. "How old are you, little girl?"

"Ten," I said shakily.

"Speak up, child. My ears are dim. Have you been a good little girl this year? Do you deserve a visit from Santa Claus? And do you make good marks in school?"

It was going to be a long afternoon.

"Yes, ma'am," I replied, feeling insulted. What did she think I was? A baby?

She shifted the cane to one hand and waved the other arm imperiously. "Sydney," she called to my mother, "have this child show me to a bedroom. I want to lie down for awhile."

It was a struggle getting Aunt Agatha up and out of her chair. Bent with age, she supported herself with a heavy hand on my shoulder. For an old lady, she sure was strong.

But my thoughts brightened as she sank onto the bed. Maybe she would sleep until it was time for her to go home.

I didn't see Aunt Agatha again for a couple of hours. Just a few minutes after she took to the bed, Uncle Bobby showed up, and we had a fine time sailing his model airplane. After a long time he said he had to go, and my mother asked me to deliver some candy to a neighbor.

By the time I returned home, Uncle Bobby was gone. Aunt Agatha was once again enthroned by the fireplace, and my presence was required. For a brief moment I was struck again by her resemblance to someone I knew.

"Your mother tells me you're studying Latin," she rasped, fixing me with a harsh stare. "Are you a good little student? Tell me something in Latin."

"Omnia Gallia in tres partes divisa est," I parroted, the only bit of Latin I could recall.

"Your pronunciation is terrible," she announced. "You must work harder. I may stay here a few days and coach you."

Inwardly I groaned as the grim picture of being tutored by Aunt Agatha floated in my mind. The old bat was going to ruin Christmas.

She turned to my mother, who was carrying a teapot on a tray.

"Sydney, I'd like this child to serve me a cup of tea. Now. One sugar and just a drop of lemon."

Mother, looking amused, prepared the tea as ordered and handed me the cup and saucer.

"And don't slosh it, child," grumbled the old witch. "I can't stand tea in my saucer. Don't be clumsy."

Seething with outrage at her insults, I started across the room with the teacup and saucer. Truly, it was an accident that my foot slipped on the edge of the rug. Horrified, I watched as the cup, the saucer and the tea flew—separately—toward Aunt Agatha. The cup landed in her lap, the saucer at her feet, and the tea soaked into her springy curls and dribbled down her face.

"Holy smoke, Mac," she yelled in Uncle Bobby's voice, using Uncle Bobby's nickname for me. "Watch out what you're doing!"

Amazed, all I could do was stare at Aunt Agatha. She began to laugh—Uncle Bobby's laugh—as she removed her tea-soaked cap, her wig, her shaggy eyebrows, her dress and her crocheted mittens. As she completed her metamorphosis, there stood Uncle Bobby, wearing the clothes he had worn while we were flying the airplane.

I turned to my mother for an explanation. She was doubled up behind the teapot, laughing so hard she couldn't speak.

I realized I was the victim of another one of my family's numerous Christmas pranks.

And each year to this day, at Christmastime we still refer to Uncle Bobby as Aunt Agatha from Hahira.

Dominus Vobiscum

Chewing gum was forbidden, and we never crossed our legs. We wore beanies to daily Mass, paused to pray eight times a day and, from the age of 6, committed the Baltimore Catechism to memory.

We were Catholic-school students in the days when Mass was in Latin, nuns were teachers and Friday meant fish sticks for lunch.

We wondered—but never dared ask—whether the nuns had hair, whether they had ever been kissed. and whether they ever wished they weren't nuns.

And, of course, we wore uniforms.

It all came back to me when a former schoolmate sent me a copy of *Growing Up Catholic,* a wonderful chronicle of days that exist now only in such books and in the memories of those of us who lived them.

The rigid rules of Catholicism were relaxed as a result of Vatican II, the ecumenical council of the early '60s, and nuns, for the most part, have vanished from the classroom. Their exodus has left a void that no one can fill in quite the way they did. No one can teach like a nun. With no families at home, no outside commitments, they devoted their lives to shaping ours—an education that covered far more than textbooks.

Actually, I grew up Methodist, but my parents believed—correctly, I think—that a Catholic education was the best available at the time. So, I entered first grade at Christ the King School and remained there until the high school closed at the end of my junior year.

We were required to meet rigid standards for impeccable posture as well as saintly behavior. Loud voices affronted our guardian angels. The Blessed Mother smiled upon good table manners.

Once I was caught biting my nails and ordered to write a 300-word composition titled, "My Body Is a Temple of the Holy Ghost." (It was far easier to give up nail biting than to think of 300 words on the subject.)

On one morning in each of our high school years, class was suspended, and we assembled for a lecture on dating. The nuns referred to it as the Assembly on Christian Morals; we called it the Big Sex Talk.

A girl of good character, we learned in the Big Sex Talk, never wore sleeveless dresses or open-toed shoes. Either one led boys to impure thoughts. Crossing the feet at the ankles was OK, provided you kept your knees pressed firmly together. Touching below the neck, including holding hands, was a Near Occasion of Sin, as was dancing too close together.

In case a boy made improper advances, we were to tell him, "I am a child of Mary." Thus squelched, he would promptly desist. "I am a child of Mary" was also effective when your date suggested seeing a movie not approved by the National League of Decency. (I think only Walt Disney films were ever approved.)

The nuns rapped our knuckles with rulers when we misbehaved. But even more effective was the Ultimate Weapon—the Ten Commandments.

Public school teachers have never had the Ultimate Weapon to fall back upon. I suspect that's why they complain about trying to keep order.

Obedience in school came under the Fourth Commandment—Honor Thy Father and Thy Mother. Profanity violated the Second Commandment, of course. Graffiti was covered by the Seventh Commandment since Thou Shalt Not Steal extended to not destroying property. Failure to do your homework was one of the Seven Deadly Sins—sloth.

Sin was the enemy, each one creating a loathsome black spot on the soul. The greater the sin, the larger the spot. We imagined our souls as white rectangles, liberally peppered with black dots in varying sizes.

To the nuns, it mattered not a whit that I was Methodist. I was there, so I got the whole program—daily Mass, Novena on Wednesdays, the Stations of the Cross every Friday in Lent and catechism every day.

The seven gifts of the Holy Ghost? Wisdom, understanding, counsel, knowledge, fortitude, piety and fear of the Lord.

Why did God make us? God made us to show forth his goodness and to share with us his everlasting happiness in Heaven.

Never let it be said I didn't memorize my catechism. If you want, I can even give you a couple of Gregorian chants and the Creed in Latin.

I wouldn't have missed it for the world. And for a Methodist, I grew up a pretty good Catholic.

History Repeats

My mother listened patiently on the other end of the line while I groused into the telephone.

I had just completed two conversations via long distance with two young ladies I know at the University of Georgia.

My conclusions from those conversations? They are frittering away their time on parties and dates. They are paying insufficient attention to preparing for the future.

"They just don't take it seriously," I griped. "They're up there having a big party when they should be studying. I don't see how they could be so frivolous."

My mother was philosophical.

"Pretty soon they'll realize they have to buckle down," she said. "Right now they're just experimenting with their newfound freedom."

Her final words on the subject were, "Don't worry."

Two days later, an envelope arrived in the mail. It was from Mother, one of her chatty, newsy letters. At the end was a postscript: "You may be interested in the enclosed note I received in May of 1961."

The handwriting on the enclosure looked familiar. I was sure I had seen it somewhere before. As I read, the identity of the writer became all too apparent.

"Dear Mom:

"Hi. Things here are really great, lots of fun. I got invited to the Phi Delt spring formal next weekend, and I don't have anything to wear. My pink dress would be OK, but everyone saw it at the winter formal.

"Would it be OK if I got a new dress? I won't spend more than a couple of hundred, and I can just charge it at Rich's if you'll send me your charge card. Please send it quick so I can begin looking.

"You could send me your Davison's card, too, while you're at it, so I can look there, too.

"Better yet, if you just sent a blank check, I could get a dress anywhere.

"The intra-sorority games were yesterday. I was on the volleyball team, and we practiced every minute for two weeks, but the Kappas beat us anyway. Now they get to keep the trophy. Rats.

"We have been playing lots of bridge in the dorm. Sue taught me the Blackwood convention, and it's neat. We are going to enter a duplicate tournament somewhere as soon as we get a little bit better. And we are going to start a bridge club on our hall. Bridge is hard, but it sure beats going to classes.

"Speaking of classes, I declared my major yesterday. I have decided to major in history. A lot of the history professors are really cute, so I'm sure history will be interesting. Even though it's hard and I've never liked it much, it will be fun to have good-looking professors for a change.

"And my history adviser is a dream. He looks like an older version of Tab Hunter.

"I'm glad you liked my English composition. I know it's the only A I've made so far, but I'm going to start studying and make some more A's soon, I promise. How did you like Professor Darsey's note at the end? I thought it was nice of him to say it was a good effort. He said yesterday after class he was disappointed I didn't major in English. He's just like you—he wants me to write. But writing is hard, and it's so boring. I don't see how you stand it. I could never be a writer. Never.

"Judy found a chicken walking by the side of the road the other night on the way back from supper, and she brought it back to the room. It's white and it has a hurt foot. We named it Precious Treasure and we're keeping it in a box in the closet. It's real sweet. I don't know what is going to happen, but we're in big trouble if our hall counselor finds it. We paid the maid not to rat on us. She said she would like to have the chicken, and I wish Judy would let her take it. To tell the truth, it sort of smells in here right now.

"Last night I went out to supper with John. You remember John. You met him on Parent's Day, the one with sort of blond ducktails who combed his hair a lot. Remember? You said he mumbled, but I think he's just trying to act like James Dean. Anyway, he traded the motorcycle for a red MG. Wow! Can it go! Tonight we are meeting some of his friends at Moe's and Joe's. But I have a big philosophy test tomorrow, so I can't stay out late. Rats.

"Please send the check as soon as you can, and thanks a lot.

"Love
"Skippy

"P. S. Where do you buy chicken feed? We couldn't find any in the grocery store."

Shoes and Ships
and Sealing Wax

"The time has come," the Walrus said, " to talk of many things:
"Of shoes—and ships—and sealing wax—of cabbages—and kings—"

—Lewis Carroll,
The Walrus and the Carpenter

With apologies to Lewis Carroll, there seems no better way to title this chapter than to use his line. A columnist ranges far afield in search of topics about which to write. The columns that follow are on a variety of subjects as unrelated as cabbages and kings.

Let's Hear It for Lord Sandwich

August is National Sandwich Month and therefore one of my favorite times of the year (next to Christmastime, Springtime, October and pay day).

I would be less than honest, though, if I tried to make you think the only time we eat sandwiches at our house is during August. We eat sandwiches every day and sometimes twice (or even three times) a day.

Sandwiches were invented by and named for John Montagu, the fourth earl of Sandwich, in 1762, in rather interesting circumstances.

John M. (E. O.) Sandwich was an English statesman and first lord of admiralty during the American Revolution.

He traveled widely, wrote many books, and was keenly interested in things naval, particularly exploration. The Sandwich Islands in the Pacific were named for him by Capt. James Cook.

As a member of the House of Lords, Lord Sandwich served on many important committees and subcommittees and is recognized by historians (who are very particular whom they recognize) as one of the great English administrators.

But despite his gifts as a statesman and committee chairman and his years of service to his country, he is best known for having thought of ordering his supper served neatly between two pieces of bread (which just goes to show that what you eat can be more important than how many committees you serve on).

The whole truth of the matter is that in his spare time, when he wasn't going around making treaties and calling executive board meetings and getting up the telephone committee, Lord Sandwich was quite fond of drinking, gambling and generally carrying on.

One night during a winning streak, he didn't want to break his luck by leaving the table, and he sent for his supper to be brought to him between two pieces of bread so that he could hold it and eat while continuing to throw the dice.

His friends were astounded by this feat of inventiveness and promptly sent out for ham and Swiss on rye with mustard and mayo and a thin slice of onion. And thus was born the sandwich.

Lord Sandwich lived for many years, discovering and inventing more different kinds of sandwiches than Howard Johnson has flavors.

He died at the age of 74, and on his deathbed attributed his longevity to a steady diet of sandwiches and gin.

Unfortunately for Lord Sandwich, he had been ruined as a political figure by the success of the American Revolution, which the Whigs said was all his fault, so he lived the remaining years of his life in poverty, able to afford only peanut butter sandwiches to eat, like many of us today.

So he was thankful that he had invented them.

And so am I. Just think of all your favorite kinds of sandwiches and you can be grateful to him despite the fact that he was something of a bad character: Salami, ham, tomato, egg salad, provoloni, pimento cheese, onion, pineapple.

Turkey, liverwurst, fried egg, chicken salad, steak, deviled ham, peanut butter and jelly, peanut butter and mayonnaise, peanut butter and banana, peanut butter and almost anything—all of these we owe to the earl of Sandwich.

I think I'll go make one now.

A Life of Crime

Last weekend, I found Ozywaddle in a box of old toys in my mother's basement, standing on his head and staring with his black bead eyes at a broken top.

He looked so forlorn that I brought him home.

Now he is sitting on my dresser, staring with his black bead eyes at the opposite wall.

I have to find something more interesting for him to do. One cannot desert the friends of one's youth in their old age. And Ozywaddle—until he hit Skid Row in the box of old toys—was accustomed to a life of high adventure.

Ozywaddle is a teddy bear, and he was my earliest partner in crime. In his youngest days his fur was crisp and golden, his eyes were large black circles of felt, and his stuffing was all there. My mother named him Ozymandias, but in my baby vocabulary the name became vulgarized into Ozywaddle.

One horrible afternoon when he was 4, he was blinded by one of my playmates who, in a fit of pique, bashed him in the head with a toy truck and pulled off both his eyes.

Ozywaddle never let this handicap get him down. He remained steadfast in his quest for reckless adventure. I can see him now, perched on the handlebars of my tricycle as I pedaled furiously around the driveway. Occasionally he fell off, landing with a soft thud on the pavement. But he always came back for more. He was tough.

He used to get his kicks being thrown out of bed every morning. And he had a criminal mind. When cupcakes disappeared from my mother's kitchen, it was always Ozywaddle who had taken them. He muddied my Sunday clothes on a regular basis and once led me into a neighbor's arbor where we burgled grapes for several hours. He never ratted on me, but my mother caught on after I was violently ill all night from an overdose of scuppernongs.

After Ozywaddle outgrew me, he tried for the straight life for several years, first on the toy shelf and later sitting placidly against the pillow on my bed, accompanied by dolls and other stuffed animals I left behind when I went to college. My mother took pity on him and sewed on the black bead eyes he wears to this day.

But about 17 years ago, he took up with my children and returned to the wild ways of his youth. He raced through the house, stole cookies, drew on walls with crayons and occasionally used a four-letter word.

I recall one time when I discovered that he had spent a long afternoon swimming in the toilet—definitely taboo. No one saw him dive in, so it was apparently all his own idea. After that, he was never quite the same, despite the fact that we removed his stuffing, washed him and dried him in the clothes dryer. His fur—what was left of it—became limp, and the new stuffing never fit just right. His interior was lumpy, his arms and legs floppy.

Undaunted by his disreputable appearance, he continued his life of crime: burying himself for a week in the sandbox, running away from home to spend the night in a tree and dropping peas and carrots from the children's plates underneath the dining room table for the dog to eat. During a brief phase, he played with matches but quit after he charred the tip of one of his ears.

Once he even lured my son into reading a *Playboy* magazine. They were "just looking at the pictures," my son explained.

Then during a move to a new house, Ozywaddle disappeared. No one could recall seeing him in any of the packing boxes, so we assumed he had left us for good. I am still not sure how he turned up in the box in my mother's basement.

But now he's back, and I'm sure he's bored. There isn't much at our house to interest a disreputable old bear. But at his age, maybe we can hope that he's ready to turn over a new leaf.

I think I'll at least get him a rocking chair.

Flee, You Flea!

This week, I learned some very depressing news.

Here it is: A single flea can produce an estimated 222 trillion offspring in its nine-month lifetime.

My press release does not say what a married flea can produce.

Actually, not one but three press releases on fleas crossed my desk this week. The Pet Information Bureau in New York sent two; the other came from the American Animal Hospital Association.

Almost everyone is interested in fleas.

Now, unless you own a dog or a cat in September, you may find 222 trillion fleas difficult to comprehend.

But this time of year, just about any dog or cat owner will confirm that 222 trillion is an ultra conservative estimate made by an incurable optimist on his most sanguine day.

Until last weekend, each of my three cats was harboring the entire family line of at least a couple of prolific fleas: an estimated 1,332 trillion tiny patent-leather suckers.

My own interest in fleas stems from the fact that when the cats came into the house, as they do whenever the door opens, they sat around scratching off fleas with reckless abandon. Then when the cats returned outdoors, the orphaned fleas remained behind to hop hither and yon in search of warm blood.

I quickly grew tired of playing host, literally, to a bevy of fleas.

So, I called up my mother, who used to raise dogs and who knows everything.

"How does one eradicate fleas?" I asked her.

"Oh, my goodness," she replied in several horrified tones. "It's nearly impossible. You'll have to have your house bombed."

This was startling news. I knew fleas were a problem, but I didn't know it was that serious. Would my homeowners' insurance cover the reconstruction, I wondered.

So, my mother explained the essentials of flea bombing.

Sure enough, on the grocery store shelf I found whole regiments of flea bombs. And countless fleas died that very afternoon.

Now that my house is flealess, I will pass along to you some additional interesting facts about fleas:

● Flea collars are of limited value, veterinarians say, since a flea spends only 20 percent of its time on a dog or cat. It jumps on for a meal and then hops off again when it's finished.

This explains why the fleas at my house were trying to spend 80 percent of their time on me.

● Some fleas can leap 15 to 36 inches high, the equivalent of a person jumping over the Washington Monument.

There are possibilities here. If we can put the fleas in training for a Flea Olympics, it will keep them so busy that they will forget all about dining on people and dogs and cats.

● There are approximately 250 types of fleas reported in North America, but the most common types affecting dogs and cats are (and this is interesting) the dog flea and the cat flea.

Remember those. Most of the fleas you will ever see will probably be of those two varieties. Other common types are living room rug fleas, front porch furniture fleas, kitchen floor fleas, human leg fleas and circularly swimming fleas.

This last type has a brief life span, having been captured and flicked into the toilet where they very shortly become maelstrom fleas and later evolve into sewer fleas.

● Here's a recommended flea test: Put your pet on a white paper towel or old sheet. Vigorously rub, brush or comb against the lay of the hair near the tail. If any small, black particles looking like ground pepper show up, put a few drops of water on them. If they dissolve into reddish-brown splotches ("flea dirt"), it's probably time to do battle with fleas.

That may be a fine test for dogs. But just try putting a cat on a white paper towel or old sheet and vigorously rubbing, brushing or combing against the lay of the hair near the tail. What you'll get will be lacerated hands and arms and not a few amputated fingers.

And now you know as much as I know about fleas.

Oh, yes, one other thing. In 10 days, I'll have to bomb the house again. That's because the fleas I exterminated will have left lots of eggs behind. Fleas always leave lots of eggs behind. And it takes these speedy demons only 10 days to hatch into hungry adult fleas.

I told you the news was depressing.

Take It Off!

May is the month when you try on your summer clothes—those sleeveless, backless, legless little scraps of cloth that rudely reveal all that weight you gained all winter.

They should declare May "National Take It Off Month," because May is when everyone goes on a crash diet in an effort to be svelte and sylphlike under the summer sun. At least I do.

Having determined finally, irrevocably and once and for all that the mirror is not warped, last year's bathing suit has not shrunk in size, and the other too-small clothes do not, in fact, belong to the children, I begin to think about deciding to maybe the first of next week go on a diet. It's a tough decision.

The Arabs and the Israelis will settle all their differences before I am able to go on a diet without first going through a week of neurosis. Deciding to go on a diet is a move fraught with nagging little no-win decisions that leave me anxiously biting my nails, smoking to excess and gazing longingly into the refrigerator.

Decision One is should I buy a few large size summer things to wear until I can get into my old ones, or should I punish myself by wearing my winter turtlenecks until I am back to my original, small (well, smaller) size?

Decison Two: Should I go on a sensible, slow, doctor-approved, vitamin pill-accompanied diet and arrive at my desired skinny state just in time for school to start again and the pools to close, or should I follow my inclination to subsist on carrots and celery until I am my ideal sylphlike self, hopefully in about a week or two?

Decision Three: What sort of exercise program should I initiate, assuming that a diet of celery and carrots alone will leave me with any exercise energy? I could try running in place, except the last time I did that the children charged their friends admission to "come in and watch Mama jiggle." I could jog to the office and back, but only if there's absolutely no alternative. I think I will just do deep knee bends while scrubbing the bathtub.

Decision Four: Should I begin the diet right now with a hearty snack of celery tops and suffer through the party Saturday night while everyone else is snacking, sipping and stuffing, or should I wait until after Saturday night, enjoy the party and go on a diet first thing Sunday morning?

Decision Five: Should I tell my family and friends I am going on a diet, or should I say nothing and wait till they notice my slimmer, trimmer profile? If I go ahead and tell them, I will have someone on hand to encourage me when the going gets tough. Also, I will be able to complain when I'm hungry instead of suffering in noble silence.

These are a few of the decisions I'm facing. Having once determined just when and how to diet, I can spurn all those appetizing edibles with the fortitude of a Mahatma Gandhi. It's just all these little pre-diet decisions that are hanging me up!

In Search
of a Tan

One of these summers I'm going to get a nice, even tan.

Last summer we went to the beach, and I decided, "This is the summer I'm really going to work on my tan."

Dutifully, I lay on the beach each day for increasing periods of time, having first carefully anointed myself with suntan oil.

It worked just fine until one day, while I was dozing, the children built a sand castle on my back.

For the rest of the summer I went around with a big, castle shaped white spot between my shoulder blades. It's sort of hard to explain to folks why you have a round white spot in the middle of your back, so I put my new halter-top dress back in the closet to save for this year.

Unfortunately, this year has started out all wrong, tan-wise.

To begin with, we planted a garden in the back yard. Row on row of string beans grew immediately, like Jack's Beanstalk. Beans are the only things I know of that proliferate faster than cats.

I was so delighted with the bean crop that I forgot all about getting a tan. One day I picked beans in a short-sleeved crew neck shirt. Result: tan arms to just above the elbows; red back of neck.

The next day I picked beans in a sleeveless, V-neck shirt. Result: burned arms to just above elbows; tan from there to shoulders; winter-white shoulders and back; blistered back of neck; red V on throat.

The next day was graduation rehearsal for Hawkinsville High School at 10 a.m. on the football field. I went to take a photo of the graduates for the newspaper. Sat on the bench one-half hour while they practiced. Result: left arm, left ear and left side of face, medium-rare.

On the following day, the squash in our garden was ready. It was a pretty cloudy day, so I didn't worry about sunburn. Wore Jamaica shorts and a short-sleeved shirt and picked squash for two hours. Result: burned backs of legs (white fronts of legs); blistered sliver across back where shirt-tail didn't quite meet shorts-top as I leaned over to pick squash; nasty disposition caused by intense pain.

On inspection, I decided I looked like a patchwork quilt. The logical thing to do was to even up the patches. So, to town immediately for a tube of quick-tan cream.

I decided to put it on my legs first. After reading the directions, I smoothed the cream on one leg and was just about to start on the other when my little girls came in and said my son had his pants caught in the chain of his bicycle at the other end of the block.

Went down the block and separated the screaming child from the bicycle (after he hopped around yelling while I hand-turned the pedals and tugged on the pants cuff).

Took the child back home—me pushing the bicycle and fuming over the chewed-up cuff on the brand new, size 8 pants. Forgot all about my leg until two hours later when I noticed it was jaundiced. Now one leg is white and one is streaky brown.

In the meantime, the cucumbers are getting ready, and there is more squash. Next time it rains, I'm going out and pick them.

You Have Won!
(Again)

The letter came addressed to Mr. Skippy Lawson, so right away I knew it wasn't from a close friend. A map fell out of the envelope.

"Dear Sir," the letter began. It went on to tell me that I have been selected to receive a valuable prize, already waiting with my name on it. My prize is one of the following: a new Cadillac, a portable color TV, a genuine mink coat, or a set of six ever-sharp steak knives.

All I have to do to claim my prize (guess which one it will be) is to travel to the coast and allow one of their representatives to take me on a tour of exclusive Ego Acres. Whether or not I care to purchase one of their attractive lots, the prize is mine absolutely free without strings attached. But I must respond by June 25 or lose my chance for my lovely gift.

The same mail brought another envelope of impressive size, this one labeled "Mailgram." "Hurry!" it said in large blue type outlined with red stars. "Reply today!" It was addressed to Mr. Sidney Lawson. Right away I knew it wasn't from a close friend. I opened it. A map fell out.

This one offered one of the following: a portable AM/FM cassette player, a new Cadillac, a designer telephone, a trip to Disney World, or a set of six ever-sharp steak knives.

All I have to do to claim my prize (guess which one it will be) is to travel to eastern South Carolina and allow one of their representatives to take me on a tour of Beehive Bonanza Condominiums. Whether or not I care to purchase one of their exclusive condos, the prize is mine absolutely free and without strings attached. But I must respond on or before June 27 or lose my chance.

In the same mail came a third envelope. This one was classier than the others, a discreet beige. It was addressed to the Hon..S. D. Lawson. Right away I knew it wasn't from a close friend.

I opened it. A map fell out.

"Dear S. D. Lawson," the letter began. "It is our pleasure to announce that you have been selected to receive one of our valuable prizes. We urge you to respond at your earliest convenience, as time is of the essence."

This one offered a new Cadillac, a hot tub, a home computer, a genuine mink cape, a 35-mm camera or a color TV.

What? No steak knives? I read on.

All I have to do to claim my valuable prize is to travel to the Florida panhandle and allow one of their representatives to take me on a tour of The Last Resort. Whether or not I decide to purchase one of their spacious beachfront lots, the prize is mine free and absolutely with no strings attached. But the favor of my response is requested on or before June 26, or they "regretfully" must award my prize to the next person on the list.

I read on, looking for the catch. I found it. There, on the bottom of page 3 in tiny letters, was this item marked with an asterisk: "Note: In the event that response to this offer exceeds our store of exciting prizes, a set of six ever-sharp steak knives will be substituted."

I have composed a blanket response to these three enticing epistles.

"Dear Sir or Madam: I am terribly excited about the prospect of receiving your valuable prize that already has my name on it and will arrive at 8 a. m. Saturday for my tour. I will be bringing my 10 adorable children, all under the age of 8, since my mother can't keep them. She is still in the hospital recovering from the nervous breakdown she had after they filled her pillowcases with fire ants. She says they are incorrigible, but really, the little darlings are just fun-loving and rambunctious. They will be anxious for a good romp after our four-hour drive, so I am pleased that you have plenty of acreage where they can run free. I trust your representative is accustomed to dealing with small children and that you have plenty of bathrooms.

"We also will be bringing our English mastiff Precious, who goes everywhere with us. Precious is an attack dog, but despite his size and training, he is quite gentle unless provoked. I trust that you have plenty of trees and/or fire hydrants.

"Looking forward to our outing together, I remain,

"Most cordially yours,

"S. Lawson

"P. S. Please caution your representative not to use the phrase "steak knives" at any time while we are there. It just happens that "steak knives" is the signal for Precious to attack, and human flesh gives him just terrible indigestion. Thank you very much."

... And Flap
Your Wings

"If God had meant for men to fly, he would have given them wings," goes a not-so-old saying.

If God had meant for me to fly, he not only would have given me wings, he would have given me an optimistic outlook, faith in the engineering abilities of my fellow man and an enthusiasm for altitude.

Instead, when I'm considering an airplane flight, my nerves coil up like bedsprings and my dreams are inhabited nightly by airplanes, all spinning vertically toward the ground.

I have talked to a lot of people who don't like to fly. Some say that the takeoff is the worst part. Some say it's the landing that gets them down (no pun intended).

As far as I'm concerned, it's all bad.

Having recently flown to Chicago and back, I have some handy hints for those who must fly but don't want to.

1. At the airport, listen to the confident voice of the flight announcer. "Good afternoon, ladies and gentlemen. We hope you will enjoy your flight with us. Your plane is now ready for boarding." Try not to think about the fact that he can afford to sound relaxed. He's not getting on the plane.

2. Before boarding, look around at the passengers who are getting on the plane with you. Find a few aggressive-looking souls. Would they be getting on a flight that's going to crash? Of course not.

3. It helps a little to watch the stewardesses, too. They look as if they never give a thought to the possibility of crashing. That is, until they get to the part with the oxygen masks and the emergency exits. Try not to think about emergencies. Any emergency that would happen on an airplane is likely to be very depressing to think about.

4. Once in the air, do not look out the windows. Looking out the windows will only remind you how far above the ground you are. For another thing, you will notice all those rows of little rivets on the wing. Then you

will start to imagine what would happen if one of them popped loose . . . and then another . . . and then another. Thirdly, if you look out the window during a night flight, you will see that all the motors are on fire.

5. If you are flying alone or with one friend, fly first class. If you fly tourist, you'll wind up next to someone in the third seat who wants you to just look out the window at the lovely clouds. It is better to sit in first class, alone or with a sympathetic friend, gripping the armrests and staring rigidly at the back of the seat in front of you.

6. By mental concentration and sheer willpower, you can keep the plane in the air. Whatever you do, don't go to sleep. If you go to sleep, you will break your power of concentration that's keeping the plane in the air, and you know what will happen then.

7. Make no attempt to move around in the plane. Airplanes are very much like canoes—any excess or sudden motion can capsize them, and you know what would happen then. Use the airport restroom before you board the plane. After all, it would be terrible to crash while you were occupado.

8. There are a number of things about landing that you should know. First, when the pilot looks down and sees the airport, he slows the plane down. You will experience the sensation of stopping in midair. I can almost guarantee you that this is not so. The engines may seem to die, and the plane may start to nose down swiftly, but all of this is planned, I think.

9. There will be a very unpleasant grinding noise as the wheels are lowered, and the plane will shudder as they lock into place. This may happen several times, but keep your cool. I think the pilots like to play with the wheel-lowering buttons in the cockpit.

10. As out of the corner of your eye you see the ground rushing up to meet you, appease the fates by clenching your teeth, closing your eyes and chanting, "I'll never fly again; I'll never fly again."

11. Once on the ground, try to ignore the fact that you are now hurtling toward the terminal at about 200 mph and if the brakes fail . . .

12. Pay no attention to the horrible noise when they engage the brakes. The noise is difficult to ignore because it sounds as if the wheels have come off and the plane is sliding on its belly, or a tornado is coming, or Godzilla is approaching, ready for a snack.

The above hints are in no way a recommendation that you fly. They are only for use in the event you have to fly. I hope they get you there and back again.